Sufis of Andalusia

Published under the auspices of the
NEAR EASTERN CENTER
UNIVERSITY OF CALIFORNIA
LOS ANGELES

Sufis of Andalusia

The *Rūḥ al-quds* and *al-Durrat al-fākhirah* of Ibn ʻArabī

Translated with Introduction and Notes by
R. W. J. AUSTIN
School of Oriental Studies, University of Durham

With a Foreword by
MARTIN LINGS
British Museum

University of California Press
BERKELEY AND LOS ANGELES

University of California Press
Berkeley and Los Angeles, California

LC 77-165230

ISBN 0-520-01999-7

Printed in Great Britain

To Marlene

Acknowledgments

In the preparation of this book I have had much help and encouragement from many people. I am particularly grateful to Dr Martin Lings for much valuable advice in all matters connected with this work. I would like to thank Dr M. Negus and Miss Diana Grimwood-Jones who read the manuscript and made many helpful suggestions. My thanks are also due to the Spalding Trust for their generous grant towards the costs of publication and to the University of Durham whose financial assistance enabled me to purchase the necessary films and photostats. Lastly, but by no means least, I thank my wife who has been a constant encouragement to me in my work.

Foreword

Ibn 'Arabī's *Rūḥ al-quds* is probably easier to read than anything else of his that has come down to us. It was translated into Spanish nearly forty years ago, but no English translation has appeared until now, and Dr Austin is indeed to be congratulated on this volume. It was also an excellent idea of his to include passages from Ibn 'Arabī's *al-Durrat al-fākhirah*, since some of these twelfth-century Andalusian Sufis figure in both works, and the two often help to complete each other. The reader will find the introduction most informative about the author in particular as well as about Sufism in general.

It is significant that in the article on Ibn 'Arabī in the new *Encyclopaedia of Islam*, *Rūḥ al-quds* is referred to again and again. This translation now enables readers of English who know neither Arabic nor Spanish to follow up these and other such references. Moreover, generally speaking, this treatise has a special place in the writings of Ibn 'Arabī and serves to correct a false impression which many Westerners have of him, especially those who tend to think of him as a 'philosopher' rather than a 'mystic'.

There is no need to introduce the great Sufi himself to the Western reader. But I would like to enrich this short preface by the following quotation which apart from its bearing on this book is of profound general interest and throws light on not a few of those seeming paradoxes which face the student of religions. It is in fact taken from a work not on Islam but on Buddhism:[1]

'In every religion, some few centuries after its foundation, one sees a fresh flowering or a kind of second youth, and this is due to the fact that the presence of a collective and material ambience realized by the religion itself creates conditions allowing, or requiring, an expansion of an apparently new kind. . . . In Islam, the period of a Saint like Ibn 'Arabī, the "genius" of his time, coincides with a world elaborated in the course of

[1] Frithjof Schuon, *In the Tracks of Buddhism*, George Allen & Unwin, 1968, p. 153.

several centuries of Islamic moulding and displays, on the esoteric plane, a very ample and profound flowering which at times verges on the initial prophetic revelation.'

It is on this 'second youth' of Islam that *Sufis of Andalusia* is centred, and the men and women who live in its pages all have their part to play in 'the ample and profound flowering' to which Frithjof Schuon refers.

MARTIN LINGS

British Museum,
July 1970

Contents

Introduction

The *Rūḥ al-quds* and the *al-Durrat al-fākhirah*

The biographical sketches which are translated here concern the lives and teachings of some of the Sufi masters of Muslim Spain and a few from elsewhere who lived from the twelfth to the thirteenth centuries of our era. The sketches come from two works by the very celebrated Sufi master Muḥyī al-Dīn Ibn ʻArabī (or al-ʻArabī), a brief account of whose life and work forms a part of this introduction.

The first and most important of these works is his *Rūḥ al-quds fī munāsaḥat al-nafs* (The Spirit of Holiness in the Counselling of the Soul).[1] This work is in the form of an epistle addressed to his old friend Abū Muḥammad ʻAbd al-ʻAzīz b. Abū Bakr al-Qurashī al-Mahdawī who was living in Tunis.[2] This work was composed in Mecca in the year 600/1203–4 and deals with three main subjects.

The first of these is the author's complaint about the many abuses and deficiencies which he considers had become apparent in the practice of Sufism in his time. The second, by way of compensation, consists of a section dealing with the lives and teachings of some fifty-five Sufis who had taught him or whom he had met. This section has been translated *in toto* and constitutes the bulk of the present work. The purpose of this section is, according to the author, to show that, despite the many abuses, there still existed many Sufis of high spiritual attainment in the world of Islam. The third part of the *Rūḥ al-quds* is a discussion of some of the difficulties and obstacles to be encountered on the spiritual path, illustrated by descriptions of some of the author's own experiences in this respect.

The work is undoubtedly a very important one in many respects: for the early life and spiritual development of its

[1] Variations of the title include: *al-Risālat al-Mahdawiyyah*; *Rūḥ al-quds fī muḥāsabat al-nafs*; *al-Rūḥ al-qudsiyyah*; *Kitāb al-quds fī*; etc. Cf. O. Yahya, *Histoire et classification de l'oeuvre d'Ibn ʻArabī, II*, Damascus, 1964, p. 446.

[2] He is mentioned on pp. 91 and 135 of the Translation. See also pp. 27 and 35.

author, for the history of Sufism in the Muslim West and, last but not least, for throwing much light on the teachings and practices of Sufism. This importance has not been overlooked by scholars, since the *Rūḥ al-quds* is among the few works of Ibn 'Arabī to have been both printed in Arabic and translated into a European language.

The work has been printed three times: once in Cairo (1281 H) from the Yahya Ef. MS 2605; secondly by M. Asin Palacios in Madrid (1939) from the Escorial MS 741, ff. 21–40; and recently in Damascus (1964) from a manuscript in the collection of the late Muḥammad b. Muḥammad al-Jazā'irī and collated with the 1281 H edition. M. Asin Palacios also translated the biographical section of the work into Spanish in a study entitled *Vidas de Santones Andaluces*, published in Madrid in 1939.[1]

For the purpose of my own translation I have relied entirely upon the excellent manuscript in the University Library of Istanbul (79a, ff. 1–103) which is dated 600/1203–4 and is autographed by Ibn 'Arabī himself who had the copy read to him and added corrections in the margins in his own hand. At the end of this copy there are no less than nine *samā'* or certificates of authenticity.[2] In view of the excellent qualifications of this manuscript I have not considered it necessary to consult other manuscripts of the work.

The second work, only part of which has been incorporated into this translation, is Ibn 'Arabī's *al-Durrat al-fākhirah fī dhikr man intafa'tu bihi fī ṭarīq al-ākhirah* (The Precious Pearl concerned with the Mention of Those from whom I have derived Benefit in the Way of the Hereafter). This work is unfortunately only a synopsis of a much larger work of the same title which Ibn 'Arabī had left in Spain or North Africa. The circumstances under which this synopsis came to be written are best described in Ibn 'Arabī's own words: 'One of the brethren in Damascus who had been kind to me, asked me to acquaint him with the contents of a book in which I recorded some of those whom I had met and benefited from in the way of the Hereafter. How-

[1] M. Asin Palacios produced many important studies on both Sufism in general and Ibn 'Arabī in particular. The most celebrated of these is his *Islam Cristianizado*, Madrid, 1931.

[2] I am greatly indebted to the researches of O. Yahya whose invaluable *Histoire et classification* revealed to me the existence of this manuscript. Cf. II, pp. 446–50.

ever, I did not have a copy of the work, having left it behind in the West. I therefore composed for him this synopsis.'[1] In the *Rūḥ al-quds* he explains the brevity of the biographical section by the fact that he had provided a fuller account of his Shaikhs in the *Durrah*.[2] The synopsis is however shorter than the section in the *Rūḥ al-quds*.

Since the *Durrah* contains much similar material, I have translated only those portions of it which do not appear in the *Rūḥ al-quds*. Many of the Shaikhs dealt with in the *Rūḥ al-quds* are also recorded in the *Durrah*, sometimes more fully and sometimes less so. Of the fifty-five persons dealt with in the *Rūḥ al-quds*, only twenty-six are to be found in the *Durrah*. In addition to these the *Durrah* gives an account of sixteen other Shaikhs, bringing the total of persons recorded in the *Durrah* to forty-two. Thus, between the two works some seventy-one persons are recorded, four of them women.

It would appear that the only extant manuscript of the *Durrah* is that to be found in the Esad Ef. collection in Istanbul.[3] Many, including Brockelmann, have confused the *Durrah* with the *Rūḥ al-quds* so that manuscripts which were once thought to be the *Durrah* are in fact copies of the *Rūḥ al-quds*.[4] The Esad Ef. manuscript is written in an untidy *Naskhi* hand and it is sometimes virtually impossible to read certain words, names and phrases. The date of the manuscript is 1006/1597–8, which means that nearly four hundred years elapsed between the composition of the original and the writing of the only copy so far known to have survived.

As regards the original and no longer existing version of the *Durrah* it must have been written sometime before 600/1203–4, since it is mentioned in the *Rūḥ al-quds* which is dated 600 H.[5] In Ibn 'Arabī's own *Fihris al-muṣannafāt*, a list of his works which he left in the hands of his favoured disciple, Ṣadr al-Dīn al-Qunawī in 627/1230, the *Durrah* is listed among those works written in the West, copies of which were still extant in 627/1230, and not among those which he had left with a friend, probably Ibn Saidabūn,[6] and which he never saw again.[7] It would there-

[1] Esad Ef. 1777, f. 75b, 1.4. Cf. also below, p. 20.
[2] See below, p. 131.
[3] No. 1777, ff. 75–113b.
[4] Cf. O. Yahya, *Histoire et classification*, I, pp. 192–3.
[5] See below p. 131.
[6] See below, p. 159.
[7] Cf. O. Yahya, *Historire et classification*, I, pp. 37–43.

fore seem possible that a manuscript of the complete work may yet come to light.

Two problems present themselves with regard to the *Durrah* in its abridged form; firstly, the problem of the date of its composition, and secondly, the question of the differences between names and statements in the *Durrah* and in the *Rūḥ al-quds*.

As for the date of the composition of the existing synopsis of the *Durrah*, it would seem from Ibn 'Arabī's reference to 'one of the brethren in Damascus', quoted above,[1] as also his reference to information he received concerning al-Rifā'ī while he was in Damascus,[2] that the work must have been written some time after he had visited Damascus, that is after the year 620/1223.

The fact that the synopsis was written so many years after the composition of the *Rūḥ al-quds*, helps to explain the several discrepancies between the description of certain incidents in the *Rūḥ al-quds* and in the *Durrah*. A good example of these is the account of Ibn 'Arabī's meeting with Ibn Ja'dūn in Fez.[3] There are also considerable differences between the two works with respect to the names given to certain of the Shaikhs. For instance, the Abū Ja'far al-'Uryanī of the *Rūḥ al-quds* is 'Abdallāh al-'Uryanī in the *Durrah*.[4]

In the case of the incidents which are slightly differently reported one can only suppose that some lapse of memory is responsible.

[1] Esad Ef. 1777, f. 75b. See above, p. 115.
[2] *Ibid.*, f. 112b.
[3] See below, p. 115.
[4] See below, p. 63 and p. 68.

Ibn 'Arabi, his Life and Work

Muḥammad b. 'Alī b. Muḥammad Ibn al-'Arabī al-Ṭā'ī al-Ḥātimī, as he signs himself,[1] was born on the 27th of Ramaḍān, 560 H, or August 7, AD 1165,[2] in Murcia in south-eastern Spain. At the time of his birth Murcia was ruled by a brilliant commander of Christian descent, Muḥammad b. Sa'īd b. Mardanīsh, who resisted but was finally defeated by the conquering Almohads.

Ibn 'Arabī came of an ancient Arab family and his father, 'Alī Ibn al-'Arabī, was clearly a man of standing and influence; he numbered the famous philosopher Ibn Rushd (Averroes) among his friends.[3] It is possible that he was the *wazīr* of Ibn Mardanīsh, but this is not certain. His family, in addition to its fine social and cultural connections was marked by strong religious tendencies. To his father's brother, who came to the Sufi Way late in life, Ibn 'Arabī devotes one of the sketches translated below. In the *Futūḥāt* he mentions two of his mother's brothers who were Sufis, Abū Muslim al-Khawlānī and Yaḥyā b. Yughān.[4] Of the former, Ibn 'Arabī records that he would beat his legs with sticks when they became tired from standing in prayer. He was reported to have said, 'Do the Companions of Muḥammad, the blessing and peace of God be upon him, think that they can have him all to themselves; by God, we will crowd in on them until they realize that they have left to come after them men (worthy of him).' The second brother had been the ruler of the city of Tlemcen until he met a holy man named Abū 'Abdallāh al-Tūnisī:

'The king (Ibn Yughān) was in fine apparel and asked the Shaikh, "Is it lawful for me to pray in these fine clothes I am wearing?" at which the Shaikh laughed and said, "I am

[1] See plate, p. 32.

[2] This date is given on p. 675 of MS. 5624 (7838) in the Yusuf Aga Library in Konya. The manuscript formed part of the private library of one of Ibn 'Arabī's closest disciples, Ṣadr al-Dīn al-Qunawī. The entry is almost certainly in al-Qunawī's hand.

[3] See below, p. 23.

[4] See below, p. 111.

laughing at the feebleness of your intellect, your ignorance of yourself and your (spiritual) condition. In my eyes you are like a dog sniffing around in the blood of a carcass and eating it with all its filthiness, but lifting its leg when it urinates lest any soil its body. You are full of unlawfulness and you ask me about your clothes when the sufferings of men are upon your head." At this the king wept, dismounted from his horse, renounced his position and served the Shaikh.'[1]

After the downfall of Ibn Mardanīsh and the occupation of Murcia by the Almohads, Ibn 'Arabī's family moved to Seville where the magnanimity of the Almohad ruler, Abū Ya'qūb Yūsuf, assured them of a place under the new regime; indeed, 'Ali Ibn al-'Arabī seems to have been taken into government service. Ibn 'Arabī was eight years of age when all these changes took place. It was in Seville that he received his formal education. At the feet of the contemporary masters of Traditional learning he studied the Qur'an, Qur'anic exegesis, the Traditions of the Prophet, Law (*sharī'ah*), Arabic grammar and composition. Many of these masters gave him licence to teach their works. Ibn 'Arabī incorporated into a list of his own works an account of the works he had studied and of the masters with whom he studied them.[2] He seems to have done well at his studies and to have shown considerable promise, since he was later employed as a secretary by the governor of Seville. At about the same time he married a girl called Maryam, the daughter of Muḥammad b. 'Abdūn, a man of great standing and influence. This wife of his not only came of a good family, but also shared with Ibn 'Arabī his aspiration to follow the Way. This sharing of a common experience is reflected in two passages from the *Futūḥāt*:[3]

'My saintly wife, Maryam bint Muḥammad b. 'Abdūn, said, "I have seen in my sleep someone whom I have never seen in the flesh, but who appears to me in my moments of ecstasy. He asked me whether I was aspiring to the Way, to which I replied that I was, but that I did not know by what means to arrive at it. He then told me that I would come to it through

[1] *al-Futūḥāt al-Makkiyya*, II, p. 18.
[2] Ed. A. Badawi, *al-Andalus*, XX, 1955, pp. 122–8.
[3] *Futūḥāt*, II, p. 278, and III, p. 235.

five things, trust, certainty, patience, resolution and veracity." Thus she offered her vision to me (for my consideration) and I told her that that was indeed the method of the Folk.'

'I myself have never seen one with that degree of mystical experience. However, my wife, Maryam bint Muḥammad b. 'Abdūn, once told me that she had seen such an one and described his state to me, knowing him to be one who had this experience. Nevertheless she did mention certain states of his which gave indication of a lack of strength in him.'

Although Ibn 'Arabī tells us that he was initiated into the Sufi Way in 580/1184, when he was twenty years of age,[1] it is clear that much of his early youth was spent in the company of the Folk and that he aspired to and indeed achieved at an early age knowledge of a spiritual nature.[2]

Perhaps the most dramatic evidence of such early attainment is contained in his own account of a meeting arranged by his father between him and the ageing and very celebrated philosopher, Ibn Rushd (Averroes).[3]

'I spent a good day in Cordova at the house of Abū al-Walīd Ibn Rushd. He had expressed a desire to meet me in person, since he had heard of certain revelations I had received while in retreat and had shown considerable astonishment concerning them. In consequence, my father, who was one of his close friends, took me with him on the pretext of business, in order to give Ibn Rushd the opportunity of making my acquaintance. I was at the time a beardless youth. As I entered the house the philosopher rose to greet me with all the signs of friendliness and affection, and embraced me. Then he said to me "Yes!" and showed pleasure on seeing that I had understood him. I, on the other hand, being aware of the motive for his pleasure, replied, "No!". Upon this, Ibn Rushd drew back from me, his colour changed and he seemed to doubt what he had thought of me. He then put to me the following question, "What solution have you found as a result of mystical illumination and divine

[1] *Futūḥāt*, II, p. 425.
[2] Many of the Shaikhs dealt with in the sketches he met in his early years.
[3] *Futūḥāt*, I, p. 153.

inspiration? Does it coincide with what is arrived at by speculative thought?" I replied, "Yes and no. Between the Yea and the Nay the spirits take their flight beyond matter, and the necks detach themselves from their bodies." At this Ibn Rushd became pale and I saw him tremble as he muttered the formula, "There is no power save from God." This was because he had understood my allusion.'

In the years preceding his initiation, as also thereafter, Ibn 'Arabī studied the mystical sciences, the knowledge of the Real, as the Sufis call them. A lot of this learning must have been imparted to him as much by example and constant association as by formal study, although many of his Shaikhs provided regular courses of study for their disciples. The ability to benefit from this learning would depend very much on the disciple's aptitude (*ahliyyah*) and spiritual state. As has been indicated, there is little doubt that Ibn 'Arabī himself was very well equipped in this respect. Among the subjects which were taught were the metaphysical doctrines of Sufism, cosmology, esoteric exegesis, the science of letters and numbers and the stages of the Way itself. In addition the disciple would have to spend long hours of every day engaged in the practices of Sufism: Invocation, prayer, fasting, vigil, retreat and meditation. In accordance with the aptitude of the disciple the learning and the practice might produce experiences of a supersensory nature which would have to be understood and controlled. Ibn 'Arabī seems to have had many such experiences throughout his life. Among these were visions, foresight, spiritual communication with the living and the dead, and powers of healing.

While still in Seville, Ibn 'Arabī would spend long hours in the cemeteries secluded from the world and communing with the spirits of the dead.

'For some time I secluded myself among the graves. I heard that our Shaikh al-Kūmī[1] had told someone that I had given up associating with the living and had taken to associating with the dead. I therefore sent to him and bade him come so that he might see with whom I was associating. When he had prayed the forenoon prayer he came alone and found me among the

[1] See below, p. 69.

tombs sitting with bowed head and speaking with the spirits who were present with me. With great care he came and sat down beside me. I looked at him and saw that his colour had changed and that he was in distress and could not raise his head because of the heaviness which had descended upon him. I smiled, but he could not smile from the strain he was suffering. When I had finished my communications, the Shaikh was relieved of his distress, turned towards me and kissed me between the eyes. Then I said, "Who is it that has been communicating with the dead, you or I?" '[1]

This account would seem to indicate that despite Ibn 'Arabī's respect and deference towards his Shaikhs, which is apparent in the sketches, a certain innate spiritual authority seems to have created a sometimes rather ambiguous relationship with some of his masters. This is supported by his account of a disagreement between him and his Shaikh al-'Uryanī[2] concerning a certain person's spiritual state. On leaving al-'Uryanī he was met by al-Khiḍr[3] who told him that al-'Uryanī was correct and not he. Ibn 'Arabī admits that he was a newcomer to the Way at the time.[4]

Of the many Shaikhs and masters who taught and influenced Ibn 'Arabī (a considerable number of whom are described in the sketches below), two attract particular attention, being women. Both of them were of an advanced age when he met them. One of them was Shams of Marchena[5] of whom he says:

'Among the Saints there are those men and women known as the sighing ones, may God be pleased with them. I met one of them, a lady of Marchena of the Olives in Andalusia, called Shams. She was advanced in years.'[6]

The other lady, with whom he spent a considerable time, was Fāṭimah of Cordova.[7]

'I served as a disciple one of the lovers of God, a gnostic, a lady of Seville called Fāṭimah bint Ibn al-Muthannā of Cordova. I served her for several years, she being over ninety-

[1] *Futūḥāt*, III, p. 45. [2] See below, p. 63. [3] See below, p. 157, n. 2.
[4] *Futūḥāt*, I, p. 186. [5] See below, p. 142. [6] *Futūḥāt*, I, p. 35.
[7] See below, p. 143. *Futūḥāt*, II, p. 348.

five years of age. . . . She used to play on the tambourine and show great pleasure in it. When I spoke to her about it she answered, "I take joy in Him Who has turned to me and made me one of His Friends (Saints), using me for His own purposes. Who am I that He should choose me among men. He is jealous of me for, whenever I turn to something other than He in heedlessness,[1] He sends me some affliction concerning that thing." . . . With my own hands I built for her a hut of reeds as high as she, in which she lived until she died. She used to say to me, "I am your spiritual mother and the light of your earthly mother." When my mother came to visit her, Fāṭimah said to her, "O light, this is my son and he is your father, so treat him filialy and dislike him not." '

Concerning his other Shaikhs at this time I will leave the details to the sketches.

While himself seeking masters, his own great learning was now recognized and he frequently discussed questions of doctrine with eminent theologians.

'In this connection is the knowledge of the divine Name the (necessarily) Self-subsistent (*al-qayyūm*). Our brethren disagreed as to whether it was possible for men to assume this attribute. I had heard that a certain great Shaikh of the order in Andalusia, Abū 'Abdallāh b. Junaid al-Qabrafīqī ,a Mu'-tazilite,[2] had denied the possibility of this. On this point I disputed with him frequently at his place in Cabrafigo in front of his students until he finally came round to my view on the matter.'[3]

It was not until he was thirty years of age that Ibn 'Arabī travelled beyond the shores of the Iberian Peninsula. In 590/1193 he went to Tunis. It was there that he first studied *Khal' al-na'lain* (The Doffing of the Sandals) by Ibn Qasyi, the Sufi leader of the rebellion against the Almoravids in the Algarve. He later wrote a large commentary on the work.[4]

[1] Heedlessness (*ghaflah*) is the opposite of remembrance (*dhikr*) and thus a lapse from true awareness to illusion.

[2] An adherent of a school of thought in Islam which taught extreme transcendentalism. Cf. *Encyclopaedia of Islam*, art. *Mu'tazila*.

[3] *Futūḥāt*, III, p. 45.

[4] Ms. Yusuf Aga, 5624 (Eski), 109–338.

During his stay he visited al-Mahdawī, to whom the *Rūḥ al-quds* was later sent,[1] and also al-Mahdawī's own Shaikh, al-Kinānī,[2] apparently on the recommendation of al-Kūmī and al-Mawrūrī.[3] Although it is possible that he met the famous Abū Madyan at Bugia, it would seem unlikely in the light of remarks made on p. 121 of the Translation, even though Abū Madyan did not die until 597/1200–1.[4] It was in Tunis that Ibn 'Arabī had another encounter with the immortal guide of souls, al-Khiḍr.[5]

'On another occasion I was in a boat in the port of Tunis. I had a pain in my stomach, but the people were sleeping so I went to the side of the boat and looked out over the sea. Suddenly I saw by the light of the moon, which was full that night, someone coming towards me on the surface of the water. Finally he came up to me and stood with me. First he stood on one leg and raised the other and I could see that this leg was not wet. Then he did the same with the other leg. After talking to me for a while he greeted me and went off, making for a lighthouse on top of a hill over two miles distant from us. This distance he covered in two or three steps. I could hear him praising God on the lighthouse. He had often visited our Shaikh al-Kinānī,[6] an elder of the order who lived at Marsa 'Īdūn, from whose house I had come that evening. When I returned to the town a man met me who asked me how my night with al-Khiḍr on the boat had been, what he had said to me and what I had said to him.'[7]

Perhaps because of the constant fighting between the Almohads and their opponents in North Africa at this time, Ibn 'Arabī decided to return to Andalusia. On the way he stayed in Tlemcen where he met Abū 'Abdallāh al-Ṭarṭūsī whose criticisms of Abū Madyan angered him.[8] Having crossed the Straits on his way to Seville, he stopped at Tarifa where he had a meeting and discussion with al-Qalafāt.

[1] See above, p. 17, and below, p. 91.

[2] See below, p. 141.

[3] See below, p. 140.

[4] Abū Madyan's name appears repeatedly in the pages of the *Rūḥ al-quds*. See below, pp. 69 and 122.

[5] Cf. above, p. 25.

[6] See below, p. 140.

[7] *Futūḥāt*, I, p. 186.

[8] See below, p. 155.

'In 590 I had a discussion with 'Abdallāh al-Qalafāṭ at Tarifa on the relative merits of the rich and the poor, that is to say, the rich who are grateful and the poor who are patient.'[1]

After his return to Seville he had yet another amazing encounter .During his visit to Tunis he had composed a poem of which he had told no one else:

'On my return to Seville, which is a three-month caravan journey from Tunis, a complete stranger came to me and recited, word for word, the poem I had composed, although I had not written it out for anyone. I asked him who had composed the lines and he replied that they were by Muḥammad Ibn al-'Arabī. Then I asked him when he had learned them and he mentioned the very day on which I had composed them, despite the great distance. I then asked him who had recited, them to him for him to learn. He said, "One night I was sitting at a session of the brethren in the eastern part of Seville, when a stranger who looked like a mendicant came and sat with us. After conversing with us he recited the lines to us. We liked them so much we wrote them down and asked him who had composed them. He said they were being composed by Ibn al-'Arabī in the oratory of Ibn Muthannā. We told him we had never heard of such a place in our country. He replied that it was in Tunis and that the lines had just been composed there." '[2]

It was about this time that Ibn 'Arabī made his pilgrimage to the shrine of Rota, on the coast.[3] On the way there he met al-Khiḍr[4] for the third time.

'Sometime after that occasion (the second meeting) I was walking along the coast with a companion who denied the miracles performed by the righteous. On the way we stopped at a ruined mosque to perform the noon prayer. As we went in there arrived a company of those who seclude themselves from men, who were also intending to perform the prayer. Among them was the man who had spoken to me on the sea

[1] *Futūḥāt*, I. p. 577. See below, p. 129.
[2] *Ibid.*, III, p. 338.
[3] See below, p. 117.
[4] See above, p. 25.

and whom I had been told was al-Khiḍr. Among them also was a man of great worth whom I had met and befriended before. I rose to greet him and he was pleased to see me and we prayed together. After the prayer . . . the man whom I have said was al-Khiḍr took a mat from the *miḥrab*[1] of the mosque, stretched it out in the air seven cubits from the ground and stood on it to perform his super-rogatory prayers. I pointed his action out to my companion who told me to ask him about it. I left him and when he had finished his prayers, asked him about his action . . . he said he had only done it for the benefit of my companion."[2]

In the following year, 591/1194, he travelled to Fez. While he was in the city he foretold the brilliant victory of the Almohad Ya'qūb al-Manṣūr over the Christian armies at Alarcos.

'I was in the city of Fez in the year 591 when the Almohad armies crossed over to Andalusia to deal with the enemy who were threatening the territory of Islam. There I met a certain man of God, one of my best friends. He asked me what I thought of the armies and whether I thought they would be victorious or not. I then asked him what he thought. He said, "God promised his Apostle, the peace and blessings of God be upon him, a victory this year . . . in His Book, which he revealed to him in the words, 'Indeed We have given you a clear victory'; the glad tidings are contained in the two words 'clear victory' (*fatḥan mubīnan*) . . . consider the sum total of the numerical value of the letters." This I did and found that the total came to 591.'[3]

By the year 592/1195 he was back in Seville, where he seems to have spent much of his time in study and discussion, including a study of the Traditions of the Prophet with his uncle.[4] It

[1] The niche in the mosque wall which indicates the direction of the Ka'abah at Mecca.

[2] *Futūḥāt*, I, p. 186.

[3] *Ibid.*, IV, p. 220. Each letter has its numerical value and a special branch of study was devoted to a proper understanding of these values and their significance.

[4] *Ibid.*, I, p. 32.

appears that by this time his reputation for learning and spiritual authority had made many whom he met excessively deferential towards him. On one occasion, at least, he tried to break his formality.

'One night in the year 592 I stayed at the house of Abū al-Ḥusain b. Abū 'Amr b. al-Ṭufail in Seville. For the most part he was very respectful and correct in my presence. With us were Abū al-Qāsim the preacher, Abū Bakr Ibn Sām and Abū al-Ḥakam b. al-Sarrāj. Their respect for me prevented all of them from being relaxed and they were all very correct and silent; so I sought a means of making them more relaxed. I therefore said to my host, "May I bring to your attention a composition of mine entitled *Guidance in Flouting the Usual Courtesies* and expound a chapter from it for you?" He said he would very much like to hear it. I then pushed my foot into his lap and told him to massage it. At this he understood my meaning and so did all the others. From then on they behaved in a more relaxed manner.'[1]

In the year 593/1196 he journeyed once more to Fez, a seat of great learning and piety, to spend time in meditation and study, as also to attend the lectures of 'Abd al-Karīm, Imām of the Azhar mosque, on the holy men of Fez.[2] He would often go and sit in the Azhar mosque to pray and meditate. On one of these occasions he experienced a strange power of vision.

'In the year 593, in the city of Fez, I was praying with a group of people in the Azhar mosque when I saw a light which seemed to illumine what was before me, despite the fact that I had lost all sense of front or back, it being as if I had no back at all. Indeed during this vision I had no sense of direction whatever, my sense of vision being, so to speak, spherical in its scope. I recognized my spatial position only as a hypothesis, not as a reality.'[3]

Another place in Fez which he frequented for the sake of

[1] *Futūḥāt*, IV, p. 539.
[2] *Ibid.*, I, p. 244.
[3] *Ibid.*, II, p. 486. By this experience Ibn 'Arabī knew that he had reached the station of Light.

meeting men of the spirit was the garden of Ibn Ḥayyūn. Here he met the Pole of the time.[1]

'In the year 593 I met the Pole of the time in the garden of Ibn Ḥayyūn in Fez. God had given me an inspiration concerning him and had told me who he was. He was with a group of people none of whom took any notice of him, he being a stranger to them from Bugia, a man with a withered hand.... The company were discussing the Poles, so I said, "My brothers!, I will tell you something amazing about the Pole of your own time." As I said this I turned to look at the man whom God had revealed to me as being the Pole.... He said to me, "Tell what God has shown to you, but do not reveal his identity"; then he smiled.'[2]

During his stay in Fez his reputation drew to him many disciples and admirers; as he says of the meeting in Ibn Ḥayyūn's garden:

'There were with us at the gathering Shaikhs of the Folk, highly regarded in the Way of God, men like Abū al-'Abbās al-Ḥaṣār, all of whom treated me with great respect; indeed the gathering was in my honour, I being the only one who spoke on the subject of the Way. Even when they discussed something among themselves they referred it to me.'[3]

His own spiritual state was now of a very high order, since he tells us that he attained to knowledge of the Seal of Muhammadan Sainthood.

'I learnt of the Seal of Muhammadan Sainthood in Fez in the year 594 where God acquainted me with his identity and revealed to me his mark.'[4]

This period of spiritual renewal was, however, brought to an

[1] See below, p. 115, n. 1.
[2] *Futūḥāt*, IV, p. 76. See below, p. 152, where the same incident is described.
[3] *Ibid.*, IV, p. 76.
[4] *Ibid.*, III, p. 514. Later he had a vision which indicated to him that he was the Seal. The title indicates that the holder is the last direct spiritual heir of the Prophet. He considered Jesus the Seal of Universal Sainthood. Cf. A. A. Afifi, *Mystical Philosophy of Muhyiddin Ibnul Arabi*, Cambridge, 1939, pp. 98 f.

end by the threat of impending persecution of the Sufis by the Almohads who suspected them of fomenting unrest. The state of relations between the authorities and the Sufis is indicated by Ibn 'Arabī's account of his dealings with the Sultan at Ceuta.[1] In the year 595/1198 he made his way back to his native Murcia, stopping on the way at Granada to call on his Shaikh Abū Muḥammad 'Abdallāh al-Shakkāz whom he calls one of the greatest Shaikhs he had met.[2]

Perhaps also on his way to Murcia he paid a visit to the celebrated Sufi school at Almeria which had been founded by Ibn al-'Arīf, author of the famous treatise *Maḥāsin al-majālis*.[3] At the time of his visit the school was being run by Ibn al-'Arīf's disciple, Abū 'Abdallāh al-Ghazzāl.[4] While he was there Ibn 'Arabī wrote his *Mawāqi' al-nujūm.*

'We have explained all the lights, miracles, grades, secrets and manifestations (accompanying the ritual ablution) in our book *Mawāqi' al-nujūm* . . . which we composed in eleven days at Almeria, in the month of Ramaḍān, 595.'[5]

Of his stay in Murcia at this time we have only a brief mention of an inspiration by which God charged him with the mission of teaching what had been revealed to him.

'I was in Murcia in the year 595 when God inspired me inwardly, saying, "Tell My servants what you have seen of My bounty to the believer." '[6]

Sometime in the same year he attended at the last rites of Ibn Rushd (Averroes) who had died in Marrakesh and whose body had been brought back to Cordova for burial.

'He died in 595 in Marrakesh and was brought back to Cordova where he was buried. When his coffin was slung on to the horse his compositions were slung from the other side to balance it. I was standing with the jurist Abū al-Ḥusain Muḥammad b.

[1] See below, p. 129.
[2] *Futūḥāt*, IV, p. 9. See below, p. 110.
[3] Ed. A Palacios, Paris, 1933. d. 1000. Cf. below, p. 66.
[4] See below, p. 101.
[5] *Futūḥāt*, I, p. 334. It was printed in Cario in 1325 H.
[6] *Ibid.*, I, p. 708.

A specimen of Ibn 'Arabī's signature as it appears in a certificate of authenticity at the end of the Istanbul University MS.

to face page 32

Jubair, the secretary of Abū Sa'īd and my companion Abū al-Ḥakam 'Amr Ibn al-Sarrāj, the copyist. Abū al-Ḥakam turned to use and said, "Do you see what they are putting with Ibn Rushd as a balance; on one side the Imām and on the other his works." Ibn Jubair replied, "Certainly I see, my boy, God preserve you." I kept the saying (of Abū al-Ḥakam) as a warning and a reminder, may God have mercy on them all, since I alone survive of that congregation. I composed some lines on the subject:

This is the Imam and these his works,
Would that I knew whether his hopes were realized.'[1]

Whether he spent the next two years in Andalusia or elsewhere we do not know. In 597/1200 however he was in the Almohad capital of Marrakesh where he spent some time with the keeper of alms, Abū al-'Abbās of Ceuta.[2] It was while he was in the Maghrib that he had two experiences, one of which brought him to an even higher spiritual degree, while the other was to change the course of his life both outwardly and inwardly. The attainment of the station of Proximity (to God) came while he was travelling and its lofty isolation affected him deeply.[3]

'I entered this station in the month of Muḥarram in the year 597 in the Maghrib. I was distracted with joy by it and found no one else in it. I felt the loneliness of isolation and remembered that Abū Yazīd had entered it with lowliness and helplessness and found no one else in it. This spiritual abode was to be my home so I resolved not to feel alone, since homesickness is the lot of every being in existence and isolation is the lot of every stranger (to the world). When therefore I attained this station and its isolation and realized that no one would recognize its validity in me, I began to explore its various aspects and characteristics. However, although I had realized this station and the special gifts of God attendant upon it I still did not

[1] *Futūḥāt*, I, p. 153.

[2] *Ibid.*, III, p. 292.

[3] 'And now are you come to Us alone, as We created you at first.' (Qur'an, VI, 95). In this station the human attributes are consumed and only God's presence remains in the servant's awareness. Cf. Ḥujwīrī, *Kashf al-maḥjūb*, p. 249.

know its name. In it I saw the commands of God descending upon me and His envoys coming down to me and seeking intimacy with me.'[1]

The second experience was a glorious vision in which he was ordered to meet a certain Muḥammad al-Ḥaṣār and travel with him to the East.

'I saw the Throne of God as though supported on numberless pillars of light, all of which flashed like lightning. Despite this I could see that it had a deep shadow in which there was an unimaginable peace. This shadow was that of the concavity of the Throne, veiling the light of Him Who sat upon it, the Merciful. I saw also the Treasure which was under the Throne from which there issued the words, "There is no power or might but in God, the Mighty, the Supreme." The Treasure was none other than Adam, blessings be upon him. Underneath it I saw many other treasures which I recognized, and beautiful birds flying about. One of these birds which was more beautiful than the others told me that I must take a companion to the East. When all this was revealed to me I was in Marrakesh. On enquiring who my companion was to be I was told Muḥammad al-Ḥaṣār of Fez who had prayed to be taken to the East. I said that I would indeed take him, if God willed it.

'When I came to Fez I asked about the man and he came to me. I asked him whether he had prayed for anything. He said that he had prayed to be taken to the East and had been told that someone would take him there. He had been waiting for my arrival since then. I therefore took him as my companion in the year 597 and brought him to Egypt where he died, God have mercy on him.'[2]

Together with his new companion Ibn 'Arabī travelled to Bugia where, in Ramaḍān of the same year, he had another vision.

He entered Bugia in the Ramaḍān of the year 597 and met there Abū 'Abdallāh al-'Arabī together with a group of other worthy men. When he entered Bugia on the above-mentioned date he relates:

[1] *Futūḥāt*, II, p. 260.　[2] *Ibid.*, II, p. 436.

'One night (in a vision) I saw myself conjoined with all the stars of the heaven, being united to each one with a great spiritual joy. After I had become joined with the stars I was given the letters (of the alphabet) in spiritual marriage. I told this vision of mine to one who would take it to a man versed in visionary lore, bidding him conceal my name. When he related my vision to the man he said, "This is a measureless ocean and the one who has seen the vision shall have revealed to him knowledge of the highest things, of mysteries, of the properties of the stars, such as will be shared by no one in his time." Then he was silent for a while after which he said, "If he who saw the vision is in this city, it can be none other than the young Andalusian who came here." '[1]

From Bugia the two men journeyed to Tunis on their way to the East. While he was there he attained to another spiritual degree, which attainment caused him to cry out with startling results.

'I attained to this degree in Tunis. When it happened I let out a fearful cry without knowing it; the cry however caused all who heard it to faint away, including the women looking down on us (in the mosque) from neighbouring houses, some of whom fell down into the courtyard, without sustaining injury despite the height. I was the first to recover. We had been praying behind the Imām and all the rest now lay smitten. After a while they recovered their senses and I asked them what the matter was. They returned the question to me and told me that I had cried out with the results I have mentioned. I told them that I was not aware of my cry.'[2]

In Tunis he stayed with his friend al-Mahdawī whom he had visited eight years earlier. During his stay he partly completed his *Inshā' al-dawā'ir*.[3]

'. . . in our book *Inshā' al-dawā'ir*, part of which we finished at his (al-Mahdawī) house during our visit in the year 598 on

[1] *Futūḥāt*, IV, p. 559 (biography). [2] *Ibid.*, I, p. 173.
[3] Ed. H. S. Nyberg, *Kleinere Schriften des Ibn al-Arabī*, Leiden, 1911.

our way to perform the Pilgrimage (*ḥajj*). His servant, 'Abd al-Jabbār, copied for him the part I had written, while I took the original with me to Mecca to finish it there.'[1]

In the same year, having bade farewell to his friend in Tunis, Ibn 'Arabī pursued his journey eastwards with his companion, al-Ḥaṣār. Spending only a short time in Alexandria and Cairo, he continued on his way alone until he arrived in Mecca towards the end of the year. Once in the Holy City the fame of the Andalusian master was not slow to spread, and he soon enjoyed the friendship and hospitality of the most influential and learned families in Mecca. Foremost among those to receive him was a certain Abū Shajā Ẓāhir b. Rustam and his sister, a lady of great piety and learning. This man had a daughter whose surpassing beauty, virtue and knowledge inspired Ibn 'Arabī to write his finest collection of poems, the *Tarjumān al-ashwāq*.[2] When the poems were later criticized by religious scholars as being too sensuous and worldly, some of his friends persuaded him to write a commentary by way of defending the integrity of his composition.[3] In this commentary he speaks of the beautiful lady as follows:

'When I stayed in Mecca in the year 599 I met there many men and women of great worth, culture and piety, none of whom were self-engrossed, despite their virtues; men like .... Abū Shajā' Ẓāhir b. Rustam b. Abū Rajā al-Isfahānī and his sister, Bint Rustam, a learned old lady, a shining example among women. . . . This Shaikh had a virgin daughter, a slender child who captivated one who looked upon her, whose presence gave lustre to gatherings, who amazed all she was with and ravished the senses of all who beheld her. Her name was Niẓām (Harmony) and her surname 'Ain al-Shams (Eye of the Sun). She was religious, learned, ascetic, a sage among the sages of the Holy Places.'[4]

While in the Holy City, the performance of the Pilgrimage

[1] *Futūḥāt*, I, pp. 98–9.
[2] Beirut, 1961. Trans. with text by R. A. Nicholson, London, 1911.
[3] Printed with the *Tarjumān*, Beirut, 1961.
[4] *Tarjumān al-ashwāq*, Beirut, 1961, pp. 7–8.

rites must have been one of Ibn 'Arabī's chief concerns. It was during a circumambulation (*ṭawāf*) of the Ka'bah that he saw a vision which marked a crucial stage in his spiritual development. He tells us that on passing the Black Stone in the eastern corner of the Ka'bah he met 'the youth steadfast in devotion', in communication with whom he attained to an higher awareness of his essential self.

'On one occasion I was circumambulating His ancient House, and while I was engaged in this, praising and glorifying God . . . I came to the Black Stone and met the eagle stone of the youth steadfast in devotion who is both speaker and silent, neither alive nor dead, both complex and simple, encompassing and encompassed. When I saw him circumambulating the House, the living circumambulating the dead, I grasped what he was and his significance and realized that the circumambulation of the House is like the prayer over the dead. . . . Then God showed me the spiritual degree of that youth, that he was far beyond all considerations of space and time. When I had realized this . . . I kissed his right hand . . . and said to him, "O bearer of tidings, look and see how I seek your company and desire your friendship." Then he indicated to me by hint and sign that he was created to speak only by signs. . . . I begged him to reveal his secrets to me. He said, "Behold the details of my structure and the order of my formation and you will find the answer to your question set forth in me, for I am not one who speaks or is spoken to, my knowledge being only of myself and my essence being naught other than my names. I am knowledge, the known and the knower." '[1]

Also while he was in Mecca there was given to him evidence that he himself was the Seal of Muhammadan Sainthood, concerning whom he had received inspirations at Fez in 594 H.

'I saw a vision of this kind concerning myself which I took as good tidings to me from God, since it had a similarity to

[1] *Futūḥāt*, I, pp. 47–8. In this vision of the 'eternal youth' Ibn 'Arabī confronts his eternal and essential self which resides beyond the oppositions of the formal worlds. F. Meier wrote a study of this vision in *The Mysteries* (Papers from the Eranos Year Books, Bollingen Series XXX), 1955, pp. 149–68.

the tradition of the Prophet in which he indicates to us his position in respect of the other prophets. He says, "As regards my position among the other prophets, it is as if a man built a wall leaving out one brick. I am that brick and no apostle or prophet will come after me." Here he likens the Prophethood to the wall and the prophets to the bricks which make it up. . . . I was in Mecca in the year 599 when I saw, as in a dream, the Ka'bah built of gold and silver bricks; but when I looked at a spot on the face between the Yemeni and Syrian corners I noticed that there were two bricks missing, one of gold, the other of silver, one on the top row and the other on the row below it. Then I saw myself being put into the place of the missing bricks. . . . I woke up and thanked God and said to myself, "I am to the other followers of my kind (the saints) as the Apostle of God is to the other prophets." "[1]

Much of his time in Mecca must have been spent in study and discussion with the many scholars and Sufis who stayed in the Holy City. It was at this time that he had the confrontation with the jurist 'Abd al-Wahhāb al-Azdī described in the sketch on al-Mawrūrī.[2] He was also active as an author since he completed four works; a collection of Traditions called *Mishkāt al-anwār*,[3] a treatise on the Sufi virtues, *Ḥilyat al-abdāl*;[4] a treatise on visions, *Tāj al-rasā'il*:[5] and the *Rūḥ al-quds*, part of which is translated below. In addition he began the composition of his enormous compendium of esoteric knowledge, the *al-Futūḥāt al-Makkiyyah*.[6]

During this period the region suffered various catastrophic afflictions. The Yemen was ravaged by dust storms, heralded at Mecca by extraordinary celestial phenomena, while Taif was struck by a virulent plague.[7]

In the year 601/1204 Ibn 'Arabī left Mecca and travelled to Baghdad where he stayed only twelve days before going to on Mosul where he spent some time in study. While he was in

[1] *Futūḥāt*, I, pp. 318–19. Cf. *Fuṣūṣ al-ḥikam*, Cairo, 1946, p. 63.
[2] See below, p. 101, and *Futūḥāt*, III, p. 69.
[3] Aleppo, 1927. [4] Trans. M. Valsan, Paris, 1951.
[5] Autograph MS. Veliyuddin 1759. Cairo, 1328 H.
[6] Būlāq, 1329 H. An autograph copy, the second in his own hand, may be found in Istanbul, Evkaf Musesi 1845–81. See below, p. 47.
[7] *Futūḥāt*, II, p. 450.

Mosul he met 'Abdallāh b. Jāmi' at whose hands he received the investiture of al-Khiḍr for the third time.[1]

'He was 'Alī b. 'Abdallāh b. Jāmi', a companion of 'Alī al-Mutawakkil and Abū 'Abdallāh Qaḍīb al-Bān,[2] who lived outside Mosul. Al-Khiḍr had invested him in the presence of Qaḍīb al-Bān, and he himself invested me in the very same spot in his garden where al-Khiḍr had invested him, and in the self-same manner.'[3]

During his stay he also composed a treatise of fifty-three chapters on the esoteric significance of ablution and prayer entitled *Al-Tanazzulāt al-Mawsilyyah* (Revelations at Mosul).[4]

It seems likely that Ibn 'Arabī may have visited Malatya in Asia Minor about this time.[5] However that may be, we next hear of him in Hebron on his way to Cairo where he arrived in 603/1206. There he spent his time with groups of Sufi friends among them al-Khayyāṭ, his brother, and possibly al-Mawrūrī.[6] The official religious atmosphere was, however, unresponsive, indeed hostile to his teachings, and it was not long before he was accused of heresy by the authorities. The movement against him might have reached serious proportions had it not been for the timely intervention of the Ayyubid ruler, al-Malik al-'Ādil, who had received a letter of commendation concerning Ibn 'Arabī from a friend, Abū al-Ḥasan of Bugia.

'The people of Egypt were critical of him and sought to have him killed, but God came to his rescue by the hand of the Shaikh Abū al-Ḥasan of Bugia; for he strove to have him kept free and interpreted his words. After he had been saved from the danger, the Shaikh (Ibn 'Arabī) said to him, "How may one be imprisoned in whose humanity divinity resides." Abū al-Ḥasan replied, "O Sir! these are the expressions of mystical fervour, and one who is intoxicated is not to be held blameworthy." '[7]

[1] This means an initiation of a direct nature not connected to any order. According to his book *Nasab al-khirqah* (Esad Ef. 1507, 87–97b) he had also received this kind of initiation in Seville (580/1184) and Mecca (599/1202).

[3] Cf. below, p. 128.

[3] *Futūḥāt*, I, p. 187. See below, p. 157.

[4] Murad Molla 1236.

[5] Certificate for *Rūḥ al-quds*.

[6] See below, pp. 91 and 101.

[7] *Futūḥāt*, IV, p. 560 (biography).

Discouraged and distressed by these developments, Ibn 'Arabī left Egypt in 604/1207 and returned to Mecca to pursue his study of the Traditions, as also to renew his ties with the family of Abū Shajā' b. Rustam.[1] He stayed in Mecca just over a year and then made his way northwards towards Asia Minor. On the way he halted in Aleppo where he gave a certificate to a copy of his *Kitāb al-tajalliyyāt*.[2]

He arrived in Konya in the year 607/1210 where he was well received, by both the ruler Kay Kaus and the people.

'The king ordered for him a house worth 100,000 dirhams. After he had been in it for a while a beggar passed by and asked him for alms, whereupon he told him to take the house, since it was all he had to give.'[3]

His great learning and spiritual powers left a deep impression on the people of Konya. His closest disciple there, Ṣadr al-Dīn al-Qunawī, says of him, 'Our Shaikh Ibn 'Arabī was capable of communicating with the spirit of any of the prophets and Saints of the past. This he could do in three ways: (1) he would call down the spirit to this world and perceive it embodied in a form similar to that which it had in life; (2) he would see it in his sleep; (3) he would abstract himself from his body and meet the spirit.'[4]

Ibn 'Arabī himself tells us of an interesting encounter with a painter in Konya.

'It is from the divine Name, the Creator . . . that there derives the inspiration to painters in bringing beauty and proper balance to their pictures. In this connection I witnessed an amazing thing in Konya in the land of the Greeks. There was a certain painter whom we proved and assisted in his art in respect of a proper artistic imagination, which he lacked. One day he painted a picture of a partridge and concealed in it an almost imperceptible fault. He then brought it to me to test my artistic acumen. He had painted it on a large board, so

[1] *Futūḥāt*, II, p. 376.
[2] *K. al-tajalliyyāt*, MS. Awqāf Baghdād, 4827.
[3] *Futūḥāt*, IV, p. 560 (biography).
[4] R. A. Nicholson, 'Lives of "Umar Ibnu'l-Farid and Muhiyyu" ddin Ibnu'l-'Arabi', *J.R.A.S.*, 1906, p. 816.

that its size was true to life. There was in the house a falcon which, when it saw the painting, attacked it, thinking it to be a real partridge with its plumage in full colour. Indeed all present were amazed at the beauty of the picture. The painter, having taken the others into his confidence, asked for my opinion on his work. I told him I thought the picture was perfect, but for one small defect. When he asked what it was, I told him that the length of its legs was out of proportion very slightly. Then he came and kissed my head.'[1]

This visit by Ibn 'Arabī to Konya proved to be of the greatest importance for the future of oriental Sufism. Ṣadr al-Dīn of Konya was his closest disciple there and received from him licence to pass on a large number of his works.[2] Ṣadr al-Dīn himself, in later years, became a major exponent of Ibn 'Arabī's teachings and has left many important commentaries on his master's works.[3] What is more significant is that he became the link between the great Andalusian master and many of the greatest representatives of Persian Sufism, notably Jalāl al-Dīn Rūmī.[4] This connection and its consequences have been studied recently by H. Corbin in his book on Ibn 'Arabī.[5]

Leaving Konya he travelled northwards together with some of his disciples. On the way they passed through Kayseri, Malatya, Siwas, Arzan in Armenia and then South again through Dunaisir and Harran to Baghdad where he arrived in 608/1211.

'I met one of them (the Rajabīs) at Dunaisir in the Dīyar Bakr.'[6]

'One of them was Buka' a spy of the people of Arzan. I knew him personally and kept company with him. He thought highly of me and saw me often. I met with him in Damascus,

[1] *Futūḥāt*, II, p. 424.

[2] The MS. 5624 (7838) in the Yusuf Aga Library in Konya contains many licences, some signed by Ibn 'Arabi himself, authorizing him to pass on his works.

[3] He wrote a commentary on the *Fuṣūṣ al-ḥikam*, Yusuf Aga, 4858.

[4] Author of the celebrated *Masnavi* AD 1207–73.

[5] *L'Imagination créatrice dans le Soufisme d'Ibn Arabi*, Paris, 1958, pp. 55–8.

[6] *Futūḥāt*, II, p. 8. See below, p. 160.

Siwas, Malatya and Kayseri and he served me for a time. He was devoted to his mother and when I saw him in Harran he was looking after her.'[1]

'When we were in the north in the months of December and January we saw that the Euphrates, when it froze, became like solid ground, so that men and beasts, indeed whole caravans could cross it while the river flowed underneath.'[2]

In Baghdad he had a meeting with a great Sufi Shaikh, Shihāb al-Dīn 'Umar al-Suhrawardī, author of the *'Awārif al-ma'ārif.*[3]

'. . . both of them bowed their heads for an hour without uttering a word to each other and then parted. When Ibn 'Arabī was asked his opinion of al-Suhrawardī he said, "He is embued from head to foot with the norm of the Prophet". When asked for his opinion of Ibn 'Arabī, al-Suhrawardī said, "He is an ocean of divine truths." '[4]

In the year 609/1212 Ibn 'Arabī wrote a long letter to Kay Kaus who had sought his advice concerning the treatment of his Christian subjects. Conscious, probably, of the crusades, which were going on at the time, Ibn 'Arabī advised him to adopt the strictest measures in his dealings with the Christians and to prevent them, at all costs, from injuring the cause of Islam in his kingdom.

'. . . One of the worst things that have happened to Islam and the Muslims, a minority as they are (in recently conquered areas), is the clanging of bells, demonstrations of unbelief and the general prominence of polytheistic teaching in your land; also the relaxing of the constraints imposed on the protected peoples by the Prince of the Faithful, 'Umar b. al-Khaṭṭāb, may God be pleased with him; that they should build no new churches in the cities and surrounding areas, nor convents, monasteries, cells or otherwise, and that they should not repair those that have fallen into ruins; that they should allow any

[1] *Futūḥāt*, II, pp. 15–16. [2] *Ibid.*, III, p. 459. [3] Cairo.
[4] R. A. Nicholson, 'Lives', *J.R.A.S.*, 1906, p. 812.

Muslim to stay for a period of not less than three nights in their churches and feed him; . . . that they should not prevent their relatives from becoming Muslims if they so please; that they should show respect for Muslims and rise to them from their seats. . . .'[1]

Although Kay Kaus had invited him to come to his court in Anatolia, Ibn 'Arabi first went to Aleppo in 610/1213,[2] and then to Mecca in 611/1214 in order to clear up the misunderstandings which had arisen over his collection of poems, the *Tarjumān al-ashwāq*. To this end he composed a commentary in which he explained the esoteric meaning of his verses.

'All our poems relate to divine truths in various forms such as love themes, eulogy, the names and attributes of women, the names of rivers, places and stars. In accordance with this we wrote a commentary on some verses of ours entitled "The Interpreter of Desires". The commentary was called "The Treasures of Lovers" (*Dakhā'ir al-a'lāq*). This we did because certain jurists of Aleppo took us to task for our claim that our verses alluded merely to divine truths, asserting that we said this only because we were associated with religion.'[3]

Whether he visited Medina and Jerusalem at this time, or whether he had visited them earlier in 598/1201–2, is not certain.

In 612/1215 Ibn 'Arabī travelled once more to Siwas and Malatya in Anatolia where he met Kay Kaus and foretold his victory at the battle of Antioch.[4] During the years 612/1215 to 616/1219 Ibn 'Arabī seems to have spent much of his time in Malatya where he gave certificates of authenticity (*samā'*) for several of his works.[5] Between 617/1220 and 618/1221 he was in Aleppo.[6]

Kay Kaus was not the only ruler to show favour to Ibn 'Arabī.

[1] *Futūḥāt*, IV, pp. 547–8.

[2] Preface to the commentary by Ibn Sawdakīn on the *Tajalliyyāt*, MS. Fatih, 5322.

[3] See above, p. 36. *Futūḥāt*, III, p. 562.

[4] *Muḥāḍarat al-abrār*, II, p. 180.

[5] One of these was the *Rūḥ al-quds*.

[6] Certificates for *Maqām al-qurbah*, Hyderabad, 1948, and *Manzil al-manāzil*, Veliyuddin, 1759 (autograph).

For some years before he died in 613/1216 the Ayyubid ruler of Aleppo, al-Malik al-Ẓāhir, treated him with the greatest honour and placed complete confidence in him. Ibn 'Arabī seems to have been given a house in Aleppo by this ruler.

'One day I had an audience with the king, al-Malik al-Ẓāhir, ruler of Aleppo . . . son of Ṣalāḥ al-Dīn Yūsuf b. Ayyūb. There were brought before him that day one hundred and eighteen cases, all of which he judged. During one of these cases I had spoken with him in favour of a man of his court who had divulged a state secret and demeaned his kingship. Despite my plea he resolved to have him executed. His aide counselled him to keep his intention secret lest I should hear of it. I did hear of it, however, and when I spoke with him about the matter he bowed his head in shame, protesting that a ruler cannot let such crimes be committed with impunity. I said to him, "You imagine you have the dignity of kingship and that you are a Sultan! By God, I know of no sin in the world which is too much for me to forgive, and I am only one of your subjects. How is it then that you cannot bring yourself to forgive a crime which is no transgression according to God's Law? Indeed your kingly magnanimity is meagre indeed." At this he was overcome with shame, set the man free and forgave him.'[1]

This close relationship with al-Malik al-Ẓāhir, as also with other rulers, must have caused much ill-feeling between Ibn 'Arabī and the jurists and theologians. Indeed, as is clear from a reading of the sketches, the official religious authorities were always ready to criticize and condemn Ibn 'Arabī for his teachings. That he himself was equally ready to retaliate in kind is indicated by his attack on the jurists in his sketch on al-Mawrūrī,[2] as also by his comments on a talk he had with al-Malik al-Ẓāhir.

'Know that when worldly desires get the better of men's souls and scholars seek positions at the courts of kings, they forsake the true Way and resort to far-fetched interpretations of the Law to satisfy the whims of their masters who require legal

[1] *Futūḥāt*, IV, p. 539.

[2] See below, p. 105.

support for their selfish purposes, even though the jurists themselves are not really convinced by their own pronouncements. One day I was discussing this subject with al-Malik al-Ẓāhir, when he ordered a servant to bring to him a certain Harmadān. When I asked who Harmadān might be, he replied, "You have often voiced your dissaproval of the oppression and wrongs which occur in this kingdom of mine, and I agree with you that these things are indeed reprehensible; but know, Sir, that each of these things is done by the authority of a jurist who draws up the decree which justifies it, may God curse them. One of them decreed for me, quoting a greater authority from his own country, that it was not necessary for me to fast in the month of Ramaḍān itself, but that I could choose any month I liked." "[1]

In the year 620/1223 Ibn 'Arabī went to settle in Damascus where he was to remain till the day of his death, except for a brief visit to Aleppo in 628/1231.[2] His long travels, his enormous literary output and the rigorous privations of his calling had all taken toll of his health. By now famous and almost universally venerated, he took advantage of the invitation of the ruler of Damascus al-Malik al-'Ādil to take up permanent residence in that city. Both al-Malik al-'Ādil (d. 625/1227) and his son al-Malik al-Ashraf, as also the legal chiefs of Damascus, treated him with great honour. Here he completed his great *al-Futūḥāt al-Makkiyyah*[3] and also his much shorter, but very important, *Fuṣūṣ al-ḥikam*, which he intended as a synopsis of his teachings. It consists of twenty-seven chapters each of which is named after one of the prophets.[4] In addition he completed his major collection of mystical poems, *al-Dīwān al-akbar*.[5]

Ibn 'Arabī died in Damascus on the 28th of Rabī' II, 638 H. (November, 16th A.D. 1240), aged seventy-six. The chief Qāḍī of Damascus and two of Ibn 'Arabī's disciples performed the funeral rites.

He was survived by two sons, Sa'd al-Dīn Muḥammad, who was born at Malatya in 618/1221 and died in 656/1258, and 'Imād al-Dīn Muḥammad who died in 667/1268. Sa'd al-Dīn

[1] *Futūḥāt*, III, pp. 69–70.

[2] *Ibid.*, IV, pp. 83–4.

[3] See above, p. 38.

[4] Ed. with commentary by A. A. Afifi, Cairo, 1946.

[5] Ed. Cairo, 1270 H.

was a competent poet and composed a *Dīwān*. He also had a daughter, Zainab, who was apparently able to answer theological questions at a very early age.

'Once when my daughter Zainab was no more than a year old, a mere suckling child, I playfully asked her a question in the presence of her mother and grandmother. I asked what a man should do if he lay with his wife but emitted no seed. She replied that he would have to perform the major ablution. At this all present were amazed. The same year I left her with her mother, having given her mother permission to perform the Pilgrimage. I myself travelled to Iraq, intending to meet my family later in Mecca.[1] When I arrived at the meeting place, I went with a group of people who were with me to look for them in the Syrian caravan. My daughter caught sight of me and cried out, "O mother, there is my father!" Then her mother looked and saw me in the distance. Zainab went on calling, "There is my father! there is my father!" Then one of her uncles called to me. When I came to her she laughed and threw her arms round me shouting, "Father! father!" '[2]

Of his wives we know of three: Maryam, whom he married in Seville and of whom nothing more is reported;[3] Fāṭimah bint Yūnus b. Yūsuf, daughter of a Sharif of Mecca, who was the mother of 'Imād al-Dīn, called Muḥammad al-Kabīr;[4] and an unnamed lady, daughter of the Mālikī chief Qāḍī, whom he married in Damascus.[5] We do not know the name of Zainab's mother or what became of her.

The title by which Ibn 'Arabi is best known among the Sufis is '*al-Shaikh al-Akbar*' ('the greatest Shaikh'). This is probably because he was the first man to express in writing that vast range of doctrine and learning which had, until his time, been confined to oral transmission and veiled allusions. In doing so Ibn 'Arabī made available an enormous corpus of teachings on a multitude of subjects, from the loftiest metaphysical doctrines to the esoteric significance of ritual ablution, including cosmology, numerology, oneirology, Sufi practice, mystical states, etc.

[1] This must have been sometime between 606 H and 609 H.
[2] *Futūḥāt*, IV, p. 117.
[3] See above, p. 22.
[4] *Futūḥāt*, IV, p. 554.
[5] *Ibid.*, IV, p. 559 (biography).

Few other mystics of any religious tradition have provided so generous an exposition of their teachings and insights. Ibn 'Arabī himself lists 251 works in his list of books.[1] O. Yahya, in his invaluable bibliographical study *Histoire et classification de l'oeuvre d'Ibn 'Arabī*, lists 846 possible titles, many of which are, in fact, apocryphal or extracted from larger works.[2] Of this huge corpus, it is a sad truth that very few have been printed, far less studied and translated. Some seventy-one of them have been printed, mostly without a critical study of the manuscripts available; thirty-three have been commented on by Muslim authors since Ibn 'Arabī's time; and a mere sixteen have been translated into non-Arabic languages. Ibn 'Arabi's teachings, which are an essential key to the proper understanding of Sufism and which would represent a formidable contribution to the study of comparative mysticism, are therefore only incompletely available to the non-Arabist.

His two most important works are the monumental *Futūḥāt*[3] and the *Fuṣūṣ al-ḥikam*; of these, only the latter has been partially translated by Titus Burckhardt.[4] For the Arabist the most readily available texts are the two works mentioned above, those edited by H. S. Nyberg in his *Kleinere Schriften des Ibn al-Arabī* (Leiden, 1919) and those printed in *Rasa'il Ibnul 'Arabi* (Hyderabad, 1948). Recently the *Tarjumān al-ashwāq* has been published in Beirut (1961) and the *Dīwān* has been reissued. For the non-Arabist there are: the *Fuṣūṣ* partially translated as mentioned above; some smaller works translated into Spanish by Asin Palacios in his *El Islam Cristianizado* (Madrid, 1931); some small works translated into French by M. Valsan in *Études Traditionelles*; and a work included in A. Jeffrey's *Reader on Islam* (The Hague, 1962). Quite clearly the task of studying and making available to a wider readership the works of Ibn 'Arabī will be a long and arduous one.

As to the way in which many of his works were composed, Ibn 'Arabī himself provides some very interesting information.

[1] A. A. Afifi, 'Memorandum by Ibn 'Arabī of His Own Works', *Bulletin of the Faculty of Arts*, Alexandria University, VIII, 1954, pp. 109–17.

[2] *Institute Français de Damas*, Damascus, 1964.

[3] Printed 1274, 1282, 1293 and 1329 AH. Written between 589/1202 and 629/1231, he copied it again, with additions, between 632/1234 and 636/1238, which copy is kept in Istanbul. The 1329 H. printing contains over 2,500 pages.

[4] *Sagesse des Prophetes*, Paris, 1955.

'In what I have written I have never had a set purpose, as other writers. Flashes of divine inspiration used to come upon me and almost overwhelm me, so that I could only put them from my mind by committing to paper what they revealed to me. If my works evince any form of composition, that form was unintentional. Some works I wrote at the command of God, sent to me in sleep or though a mystical revelation.'[1]

He tells of times when the inspiration was so strong that he could not stop writing until the book was finished. It is said that while engaged in writing the *Futūḥāt* he would fill three notebooks a day, no matter where he happened to be.[2] He claimed that the *Fuṣūṣ* had been revealed to him in a single dream and that the *Ḥilyat al-abdāl* was written in the space of an hour.[3]

Although the student of Ibn 'Arabī faces the enormous labour of reading the multitude of his compositions and, more difficult, of understanding mystical doctrines expressed in a very abstruse and technical manner, he is very fortunate in that not a few of Ibn 'Arabī's works survive in his own hand, while many more exist in copies made with his authority. Most of the autograph manuscripts are in Istanbul, Konya and Baghdad.[4]

The very great significance of Ibn 'Arabī for the history of Sufism rests on two things: firstly, he was the bridge or link between two historical phases of Islam and Sufism; secondly, he was the link between Western and Eastern Sufism.

Ibn 'Arabī gave expression to the teachings and insights of the generations of Sufis who preceded him, recording for the first time, systematically and in detail, the vast fund of Sufi experience and oral tradition, by drawing on a treasury of technical terms and symbols greatly enriched by centuries of intercourse between the Muslim and Neo-Hellenistic worlds. To a Muslim world shortly to be dealt a crushing blow which was

[1] Introduction to the 'Memorandum', *ibid.*
[2] Maqarrī, *Nafḥ al-ṭīb*, I, Leiden, 1855–61, p. 570.
[3] 'Memorandum', *ibid.*
[4] O. Yahya, *Histoire et classification*, I, p. 78. The collection of works contained in Yusuf Aga 4868 is not, however, in Ibn 'Arabī's hand. The opening lines of the *Ḥilyat al-abdāl* in this copy read, 'Our master, our Imam, Shaikh . . . Muhyi al-Din Ibn al-'Arabī said . . .' (p. 74, 1. 4).

to leave it culturally, politically and economically weakened, Ibn 'Arabī left a definitive statement of Sufi teachings, as also a full record of Islam's esoteric heritage. In doing this he profoundly influenced all subsequent Sufi teaching and thus stands as the most important link between the Sufis who went before him and those who came after him. This is perhaps partly the significance of his claim to have been the Seal of Muhammadan Sainthood in so far as he may be said to have been the last of those to receive directly the, so to speak, unformulated teachings of the Way, while all who came after him received it through the filter of his synthetic expression.

It was because he was also the link between Eastern and Western Sufism, and that at a particularly important time, that his influence was so profound and widespread. The link was forged, as we have mentioned above, during Ibn 'Arabī's visit to Konya in 607/1210, when he took as his disciple Ṣadr al-Dīn al-Qunawī. It was through the latter's links with some of the most eminent Persian Sufis that Ibn 'Arabī's teaching reached the East. Suffice it to say that he was master to Quṭb al-Dīn al-Shīrāzī, the notable commentator on the Ishrāqī philosophy of Suhrawardī,[1] and Fakhr al-Dīn al-'Irāqī, the great mystical poet, and an intimate friend of Jalāl al-Dīn Rūmī, author of the monumental verse compendium of Sufi lore, the *Masnavi*.[2] A century later the teachings of Ibn 'Arabī inspired another great mystical writer, 'Abd al-Karīm al-Jīlī,[3] who wrote *al-Insān al-Kāmil*.

This influence of Ibn 'Arabī was not limited to the theoretical side of Sufism, but penetrated deeply into the fabric of Sufi life as a whole. Through Rūmī in the East and Abū al-Ḥasan al-Shādhilī in the West, two of the greatest Sufi orders were permeated by his teachings. In outward terms an indication of his influence is the large number of commentaries which have been written on his works, as also the still urgent debates in theological circles as to the validity or otherwise of his teachings.

[1] d. 1191 Cf. S. H. Nasr, *Three Muslim Sages*, Harvard, 1964, ch. II.

[2] d. 1273. Trans. R. A. Nicholson, 8 vols, London, 1925–40.

[3] d. *c.* 1410. Cf. R. A. Nicholson, *Studies in Islamic Mysticism*, Cambridge, 1921, pp. 77–148. Extracts from *al-Insān al-Kāmil*, trans. T. Burckhardt, Cairo, 1939, Alger/Lyon, 1953.

The Sufi Way[1]

'Men whom neither trading nor selling diverts from the remembrance of God (*dhikr Allāh*). . . .'[2]

With these words the Qur'an indicates the existence of a small group of the Prophet's followers who renounced the rewards of this world in favour of a life of prayer and contemplation more intense and all-embracing than that of the rest of the community of believers.[3] It is these men who have been, after the Prophet himself, an example and an inspiration down the ages to many generations of Muslims whose special calling and dedication brought them the name of Sufi. As with those early followers, so also with later generations the Book of God and the norm of His Prophet were the springs from which they cultivated their spiritual life. Despite some appearances and opinions to the contrary, one need look no further than the Qur'an and the Traditions to find the foundations of Sufi teaching, practice and inspiration.[4]

Down the centuries the Sufis have striven to keep alive that essential and immediate experience of divine truth which filled those first *fuqarā'* (poor in God) who lived beside the Prophet and received through his mouth the words of God.[5] As such they have been the leaven of the Muslim community as a whole, especially in troubled and chaotic times.[6] Externally they were

[1] Cf. M. Ling's excellent article, 'Sufism', in *Religion in the Middle East*, II, Cambridge, 1969, pp. 253–69.

[2] Qur'an, XXIV, 37.

[3] The Prophet himself, whose mission involved him also in the affairs of the world, is reminded in the Qur'an of the importance of this group, 'And bear with those who call on their Lord, morning and evening, seeking His good pleasure. . . .' (Qur'an, XVIII, 28).

[4] Evidence of this may be found in any Sufi work, from the earliest times to the present day.

[5] Cf. Qur'an, II, 273, '(Charity) is for the poor who are confined in the way of God . . . the ignorant man thinks them to be rich on account of their restraint. You can recognize them by their mark (*sīmāhum*).' In the chapter 'The Victory' this word is used of the mark made by frequent prostration.

[6] During the recent centuries of Muslim political decline Sufism became a powerful instrument of spiritual cohesion.

also, as in the case of the celebrated al-Ghazālī, the champions of Islam's doctrinal integrity.[1]

It is in the nature of things that the need to communicate and express an experience becomes necessary as soon as there is the danger of losing it. This is no less true for Islam in general and Sufism in particular. One Sufi of the tenth century went so far as to say, 'Today Sufism is a name without a reality, but formerly it was a reality without a name.'[2] Although this is undoubtedly an exaggeration, it is certainly true that the Sufis began to express their experience only slowly until, by the time of Ibn 'Arabī, this expression had become elaborate and detailed. Despite this, however, the most important communication of essentially inexpressible truths continued to lie in personal contact between disciple and master.

'All that is in the earth is perishing, but there abides the face of thy Lord, full of majesty and bounty.'[3]

This verse of the Qur'an, from which the Sufis have derived so much inspiration, illustrates the fundamental teaching of the Sufis which is: There is no reality but the Reality (God), and that all other realities are purely relative to and dependent upon His reality.[4] All cosmic determinations, whether formal or formless, subtle or gross, are nothing but indications (*āyāt*) of the Reality from which they stem by a process of creation or Self-manifestation.[5] Furthermore, this Reality has revealed itself, from time to time, quite independently of human will or effort, in order to instill into the creatures an awareness of their true origin and essential nature.

'Praise be to God, Lord of the worlds.'[6]

[1] Recent researches by G. Makdisi have revealed that those champions of Islam, often thought of as enemies of Sufism, like Ibn al-Jawziyyah, were in fact Sufis themselves.

[2] Ḥujwīrī, *Kashf al-maḥjūb*, p. 44.

[3] Qur'an, LV, 26. From this verse derives Sufi teaching concerning *fanā'* (extinction) and *baqā'* (subsistence), as also concerning the two poles of divine manifestation.

[4] By far the best introduction to Sufi doctrine is T. Burckhardt's *An introduction to Sufi Doctrine*, Lahore, 1959.

[5] 'Wheresoever you turn, there is the face of God.' (Qur'an, II, 115).

[6] Qur'an, I, 1. Cf. F. Schuon's study of the Sufi view of the universe in his *Dimensions of Islam*, chapters II and XI.

As regards the universe or cosmos, the Sufi, while aspiring to see beyond and through its multitude of forms, regards it as being far more than the material order accessible to the senses. For him it is a manifestation of God comprising many worlds or planes of being, numberless gradations of form and spiritual potency, superior or inferior according to the measure of their consciousness or unconsciousness of the unique Reality.[1]

'Surely We created man in the very best formation, then we rendered him the lowest of the low.'[2]

For the Sufi, as also for other religions, man is unique in creation,[3] being the central manifestation who comprises in his being all the realities and levels of the cosmos. He is the microcosm, the synthesis of the macrocosm. In addition he partakes, whether actually or potentially, of divine realities and is thus the link (*barzakh*) between the creation and the Creator, between purely relative reality and the Absolute Reality. As God's vice-regent (*khalīfah*) in the universe and as being pre-eminently fitted to receive God's commands, he is placed under the obligation (*taklīf*) to acknowledge the Source of his being and realize his true nature.

'Say God and leave them floundering in the confusion.'[4]

This dramatic command from the pages of the Qur'an indicates vividly the call which summons each Sufi from within to follow the Way (*ṭarīq*, *ṭarīqah*) which leads him away from the domain of the ego, with its extensions and projections, to the realization of his essential identity (*waḥdat al-wujūd*) with God, in recognition of the truth that 'there is no refuge from God but in Him.'[5] This aspiration is inspired by an overwhelming con-

[1] According to this view the principle of evil represents, so to speak, the insolent defiance and self-assertion of relative being and its arrogation to itself of a quasi-absolute quality. Thus Ibn 'Arabī derives the Arabic word for Satan (*Shaiṭān*) from the root meaning 'to be distant', that is, distant from the Reality, on the edge of nothingness.

[2] Qur'an, XCV, 4.

[3] That is, man made in God's image (*'alā ṣūratihi*). In times past it was the true man, as reflected in the Saint, who was regarded as the norm, fallen man being regarded as having deviated from that norm.

[4] Qur'an, VI, 92.

[5] Qur'an, IX, 118.

sciousness that God is the Absolute Reality, and by an annihilating awareness of man's nothingness and unworthiness,[1] which together produce a desire to seek direct knowledge of that Reality and to remove, by God's grace, all obstacles and veils which obscure that knowledge.

The supreme obstacle which towers before the aspirant is none other than his own ego consciousness, the 'soul which commands evil' (*al-nafs al-ammārah bi-'l-sū'*), that peculiarly resilient and persistent complex of ever-shifting images and impressions which binds us to the world of multiple forms with the chains of desire and aversion, that compound of memories and hopes which enslaves us in time and space.[2]

An awareness of his true situation and a determination to turn towards God are, however, useless without the grace of God to aid and protect him; '. . . and but for God's bounty and mercy . . .', 'God guides to His light whom He pleases'.[3] Thus the aspirant must become empty of himself and receptive to the inflow of divine grace.[4] This grace may come to him directly as inspiration and flashes of insight, or indirectly through the scriptures and rites which, as vehicles of grace, serve the seeker as guides and supports.[5] For, in addition to the task of combating his own spiritual blindness and insensibility, the aspirant must wage war against a host of external forces and tendencies which resist and fight the Spirit.[6] The Prophet once said, 'We are returning from the lesser war (*jihād*) to the greater war.'

Many Sufis have spoken of three main stages or phases in the following of the Way. Each of these stages may be said to have a passive and an active aspect, an aspect of awareness and receptivity and an aspect of aspiration and action by God's grace.

[1] 'Was there not a time when man was nothing worthy of mention?' (Qur'an, LXXVI, 1).

[2] When the Shaikh al-'Alawī had, in his youth, charmed a snake for the Shaikh al-Būzīdī, the latter made him realize that his own soul was a far more dangerous thing and even more difficult to subdue. M. Lings, *A Sufi Saint of the Twentieth Century*, London, 1971, p. 52. In the face of worldly temptation the ego is weak and pliant, but when challenged with the truth of its relativity it resists with tenacity and cunning.

[3] Qur'an, XXIV, 35, and II, 64.

[4] This is *vacare Deo* in the writings of the Christian mystics.

[5] 'And seek aid through patience and prayer' (Qur'an, II, 45); 'And we have revealed of the Qur'an that which is a healing and a mercy to the believers' (Qur'an, XVII, 82).

[6] Cf. Ephesians, VI, 12: Qur'an, VII, 17.

The first stage is that of the awareness of one's nothingness and the battle with the ego, described above. In this stage the servant is fearful before the rigour and majesty of God and experiences a state of spiritual contraction (*qabḍ*) which causes him to recoil from all which would foster his forgetfulness of God (*ghaflah*). He submits to the irresistible power and action of God (*al-qahr*) in which he seeks refuge from the world and the Devil.

The second stage is one of hope (*rajā'*) in God's bounty (*ikrām*) and wonder at His beatuy (*jamāl*). It is also the stage of complete devotion (*tabtīl*) and faith (*īmān*). This is the point at which man realizes himself as the perfect microcosmic reflection of God, true servant towards Him and true lord in respect of his central position in the cosmic order. The one who has realized this position is the Saint, the human norm through whom divine grace is chanelled into the world.[1]

In the third stage, that of knowledge and identity,[2] the essence of man is at once annihilated in and identified with the Absolute Reality. In one sense his subjectivity is annihilated in the all-exclusive ipseity of Him Who alone is, while in another sense his objectivity is absorbed into the all-embracing 'I'ness of God.[3]

The Way is also seen as being made up of spiritual stations (*maqāmāt*) and states (*aḥwāl*). The stations are, so to speak, grades which indicate the achievement of certain spiritual virtues, not merely in the ethical sense, but as modalities of divine qualities. Abū Naṣr al-Sarrāj lists seven of these stations: Repentance (*tawbah*), Self-restraint (*wara'*), Abstinence (*zuhd*), Poverty (*faqr*), Patience (*ṣabr*), Reliance (*tawakkul*) and Acceptance (*riḍā*). Once attained, these remain permanent conditions of the soul.[4]

[1] These are the ones described in the Qur'an as 'the foremost' (Qur'an LVI, 10) and 'those brought nigh' (Qur'an LVI, 11).

[2] The three stages correspond to the Hindu division of the spiritual path into the way of Action (*karma*), the way of Devotion (*bhakta*) and the way of Gnosis (*jnana*). It corresponds also to the ternary, Law (*sharī'ah*), Way (*ṭarīqah*) and Truth (*ḥaqīqah*).

[3] 'What then is there apart from the Truth but vanity?' (Qur'an, X, 32): 'He is God, the One, the Overwhelming' (Qur'an, XII, 39). In the first, as relative being, he is annihilated (*fanā'*), while in the other, as divine essence, he subsists (*baqā'*).

[4] *Kitāb al-luma'*, London, 1911, pp. 41–53.

The spiritual state, on the other hand, is generally regarded as a temporary phenomenon which comes upon the aspirant as an indication of his own particular progress on the Way. al-Sarrāj lists some of these states of soul: Self-vigilance (*murāqabah*), Proximity (*qurb*), Love (*maḥabbah*), Fear (*makhāfah*), Hope (*rajā'*), Lodging (*shawq*), Intimacy (*uns*), Tranquility (*iṭmi'nān*), Contemplation (*mushāhadah*) and Certainty (*yaqīn*). These states do not come as a result of the servant's efforts, but by God's grace alone, to aid and guide him.[1]

'Invoke the Name of thy Lord and devote yourself to Him with complete devotion.'[2]

Awareness and right knowledge constitute only one pole of the Way, its compliment being right action, the very essence of which is, according to the Sufis, the remembrance or Invocation of God's Name (*dhikr ism Allāh*), whether as the specific repetition of the divine Name in ejaculatory prayer, or in any of the other rites of Islam whose purpose is to turn man's thoughts, feelings and sensations towards God. That the Invocation of the Name is the rite *par excellence* is indicated by the Qur'an: 'Prayer indeed prevents lustful acts and grave sins, but the Invocation of God is greater' (XXIX, 45). Since, for the Sufi, consciousness of the real is nothing other than the constant remembrance of God, all else promotes nothing but illusion or forgetfulness of the real (*ghaflah*). As the Prophet said, 'This world and all it contains is accursed except the Invocation of God.' Ultimately of course, since 'there is no reality save the Reality' (*lā ilāha illā Allāh*), 'the world and all it contains' is nothing other than a manifestation of God which, to those advanced in the Way, is no longer a veil and an obstacle, but a revelation of His truth.[3] The Qur'an both adduces the world as evidence of God's bounty and warns against the insidious magic of its illusion. One must eventually see God in all things and all

[1] Cf. C. Rice's study of the stations and the states in his *The Persian Sufis*, London, 1964, ch. IV and V.

[2] Qur'an, LXXIII, 8.

[3] 'Men with knowledge of God do not run away from things as others do, for they contemplate their Lord in everything', *Letters of a Sufi Master* (al-Darqāwī) trans. T. Burckhardt, London, 1969, p. 32.

things in God so that all things show to the traveller His face.[1]

As Muslims the Sufis naturally perform all the other rites of Islam, the significance of which they interpret more profoundly. These rites lead for them either to the 'sleep of the self' in submission to God, or the 'wake of the heart' in affirmation of our true nature. Hence, the ablution means not merely the washing away of external or even internal impurity, but the purifying of the heart of all that is other than God. The prostration becomes a symbol of one's extinction before God's Reality (*fanā'*), and the sitting (*julūs*) the symbol of one's subsistence in Him as being essentially one with Him.

The same applies to the Fast of Ramaḍān which is regarded as a period of spiritual renewal, an opportunity to kill the ego through the realization of complete indigence (*faqr*) before God. During the last days of Ramaḍān many Muslims spend long periods in the mosques in prayer and religious devotions. With the Sufis this practice of *i'tikāf* is extended to become a regular practice of retreat (*khalwah*) in which the disciple secludes himself away from men and the world for the purposes of Invocation and meditation.[2] Some orders stress this practice more than others. Of the same kind is the custom of spending part of the night, or all of it, in prayer.[3] This practice of *tahajjud* is mentioned often in the Translation below.[4]

'Those who swear allegiance to you do but swear their allegiance to God. The hand of God is over their hands.'[5]

Although the oral teaching and *barakah*[4] of the Prophet had been passed down from master to disciple from the earliest times it was not until the twelfth century that groups of disciples began to form themselves into orders for the purpose of perpetuating the teachings and method of a particular master.

[1] *Dhikr* corresponds to the practice of the Jesus Prayer in Eastern Christianity, *Japa yoga* in Hinduism and *Nembutsu* in Buddhism. In most religions the disciple is warned not to practise such invocation except under the guidance of a master.

[2] This practice is inspired by that of the Prophet who used often to seclude himself for long periods.

[3] 'Keep vigil all the night save a little' (Qur'an, LXXIII, 2).

[4] See below, p. 86.

[5] This has been defined as 'a beneficent force, of divine origin, which causes superabundance in the physical sphere and prosperity and happiness in the psychic order'.

Among the earliest and most famous orders which have survived to the present day are the Qadiriyyah, founded by 'Abd al-Qādir al-Jīlānī,[1] the Mevlevis, founded by Jalāl al-Dīn Rūmī,[2] and the Shādhilliyyah, founded by Abū al-Ḥasan al-Shādhilī.[3] These orders were in no way sects of Islam nor even of Sufism itself, but rather a variety of groupings providing for a variety of spiritual temperaments. The various orders manifest different ways of association, of teaching and of practice, without thereby departing from the fundamentals.[4] A genuine Sufi order may be distinguished by its conformity to the orthodox tenets and rites of Islam, its reliance on the Qur'an and the Traditions for its inspiration and its proven connection, by initiation, with the chain (*silsilah*) of masters going back to the Prophet.

The original orders mentioned above gave rise, with the passage of time, to a large number of branch orders. The founding of these branches occurred when some Shaikh of great spiritual power and understanding advocated some new emphasis in doctrine or method and was supported in this by a group of disciples who felt drawn to his person. Among the many branches of the Shādhiliyyah order, for example, is the widespread Darqāwiyyah, founded by al-'Arabī al-Darqāwī,[5] who introduced a more rigorous discipline into the Shādhilī practice of his time. Over a hundred years later a Darqāwī Shaikh, Aḥmad al-'Alawī,[6] founded his own branch which lays greater emphasis on the practice of retreat (*khalwah*).

As indicated by the quotation from the Qur'an above, membership of a Sufi order is obtained by binding oneself by oath to the head or Shaikh of an order or, if the two do not coincide, to a spiritual master who is himself attached to the *silsilah*. This oath is inspired by the oath given to the Prophet

[1] d. AD 1166. He is one of the most famous Sufis and many orders trace their spiritual descent through him.

[2] Author of the monumental *Masnavi* (see above, p. 49). d. AD 1273.

[3] d. AD 1258. Probably the most influential Sufi master in the Islamic West.

[4] In this respect the Sufi orders are not unlike the monastic orders in Christendom.

[5] d. AD 1823. A collection of his letters has been recently translated by T. Burckhardt: *Letters of a Sufi Master*, London, 1969.

[6] d. AD 1934. M. Lings has written a fine study of this Shaikh: *A Sufi Saint of the Twentieth Century*, London, 1971, which, apart from its particular interest, is one of the best accounts of Sufi teaching and practice available in a European language.

by his companions at Ḥudaibiyah. No Sufi would think of performing any of the practices of Sufism unless he had been properly initiated into them. In many cases the Shaikh of an order is simply the elected or hereditary leader of the order who is content to maintain the existence, teaching and practice of the order. Sometimes, however, the members of an order may be fortunate enough to have at their head a Shaikh who is also a spiritual guide (*murshid*) with the power to advance his disciples along the Way in addition to the communication of the invocation.[1]

In most cases the Shaikh of an order has a deputy (*khalīfah, nā'ib*) who represents him in the event of absence or illness. If the order is a large one it may be necessary to appoint other functionaries, such as treasurer, novice-master, etc.[2] When the order is divided into several widely separated cells or *zāwiyahs*, the Shaikh appoints to each of them a *muqaddam*[3] who acts in his name and on his advice, being permitted to receive new members and counsel existing ones. In many cases the *muqaddam* himself has a deputy.

The way in which an order or its *zāwiyahs* is constituted varies considerably from order to order and depends, to some extent, upon local circumstances. Sometimes the members will live together with their Shaikh in community, while in other circumstances only the special disciples of the Shaikh would live with him. In certain situations the members might pursue normal working lives in the world at large and only meet from time to time with the Shaikh to perform the rites of the order. Frequently, in addition to the fully initiated members of an order, there might be attached to it a large number of people who have received only the 'initiation of blessing', people who do not feel able to follow the Way, but who wish to partake of the *barakah* of the order and its Shaikh.

Fully initiated members are those men or women who have

[1] If a disciple wishes to make progress in the Way he must, by God's grace, find a master with the aid of whose experience and wisdom he may avoid the many pitfalls and dangers involved in such a quest, just as the Hindu aspirant must find a *guru* if he is to reach his goal.

[2] Cf. L. Rinn's useful work, *Marabouts et Khouan*, Alger, 1884.

[3] It is possible that the office of *muqaddam* is inspired by Mus'ab b. 'Umair who was sent by the Prophet to Medina to instruct the new converts in the teachings and rites of Islam.

submitted themselves completely to the direction of the Shaikh and whose main aim in life is the realization of divine truth. They undertake to perform all the required rites and practices of the order and consider it part of their duty to serve the Shaikh in any way possible. While pledging themselves to poverty and obedience, however, they are not required to observe celibacy. As in most spiritual communities the relationship of the members to each other and to their Shaikh is governed by a code of conduct (*adab*). In the case of a community this code amounts to a 'Holy Rule' quite as strict as that to be found in any monastic community.

Each *zāwiyah* of an order meets together at regular intervals for a session (*majlis*) at which the members as a community perform the *dhikr* and the litanies (*wird*) of the order as well as the usual prayer rite of Islam. The litanies, as also the *dhikr* are often said with the aid of a rosary (*subḥah*) of ninety-nine beads. A meal eaten in silence or while listening to passages from Sufi writings may be part of the *majlis*. The performance of the *dhikr* may be accompanied by music or recited poetry. Some orders perform the *dhikr* with rhythmic movements as a sacred dance.

Women members do not join with the men in these activities, but perform them separately, usually under the wife of the Shaikh. They are however directly supervised by the Shaikh himself in spiritual matters.

The Translation

1 ABU JA'FAR AL-'URYANI of Loule[1]

This master came to Seville when I was just beginning to acquire knowledge of the Way.[2] I was one of those who visited him. When I met him for the first time I found him to be one devoted to the practice of Invocation.[3] He knew, immediately he met me, the spiritual need that had brought me to see him.

He asked me, 'Are you firmly resolved to follow God's Way?' I replied, 'The servant may resolve, but it is God Who decides the issue.' Then he said to me, 'If you will shut out the world from you, sever all ties and take the Bounteous alone as your companion, He will speak with you without the need for any intermediary.' I then pursued this course until I had succeeded.

Although he was an illiterate countryman, unable to write or use figures, one had only to hear his expositions on the doctrine of Unity to appreciate his spiritual standing. By means of his power of Concentration[4] he was able to control men's thoughts, and by his words he could overcome the obstacles of existence. He was always to be found in a state of ritual purity, his face towards the *qiblah*[5] and continuously invoking God's Names.

Once he was taken captive, along with others, by the Christians.[6] He knew that this would happen before it took place and he accordingly warned the members of the caravan in which he was travelling that they would all be taken captive on the next day. The very next morning, as he had said, the

[1] Cf. *Futūḥāt*, I, p. 186; II, p. 177; III, p. 539, where he is called Abū al-'Abbās. In the *Durrah* he is called 'Abdallāh (see below, p. 68).

[2] He must have come to Seville before the year 580/1184. Cf. *Futūḥāt*, II, p. 425.

[3] See Introduction, p. 55.

[4] The power of Concentration (*himmah*) which results from the achievement of certain stages of spiritual consciousness, makes it possible to exert control at various levels of existence. This may produce effects of a miraculous kind. Cf. T. Burkchardt, *Introduction to Sufi Doctrine*, Lahore, 1959.

[5] Both ritual purity and the facing towards the *qiblah* (Mecca) are necessary conditions for the proper performance of the prayer rite (*ṣalāh*). Cf. below, p. 86.

[6] By the middle of the twelfth century, Muslim power extended over little more than Andalusia which suffered constant incursions, great and small, by Christian bands from the north.

enemy ambushed them and captured every last man of them. To him, however, they showed great respect and provided comfortable quarters and servants for him. After a short time he arranged his release from the foreigners for the sum of five hundred dinars and travelled to our part of the country.[1]

When he had arrived it was suggested to him that the money be collected for him from two or three persons. To this he replied, 'No! I would only want it from as many people as possible; indeed, were it possible I would obtain it from everyone in small amounts, for God has told me that in every soul weighed in the balance on the Last Day there is something worth saving from the fire. In this way I would take the good in every man for the nation of Muḥammad.'

It is also told of him that, while he was still in Seville, someone came and informed him that the people living in the fortress of Kutāmah[2] were in desperate need of rain, begging him to go there and pray for them, so that God might bring them rain.

Although there lay between us and the fortress the sea and an eight-day journey overland, he set off with a disciple of his named Muḥammad. Before they set off someone suggested to him that it would be enough for him to pray for them without travelling to the fortress. He replied that God had commanded him to go to them in person.

When they had finally reached the fortress they found themselves barred from entering it. Nevertheless, unknown to them, he prayed for rain for them and God sent them rain within the hour. On his return he came to see us before going into the city. His disciple Muḥammad later told us that when God had sent the rain it had fallen on all sides of them but that not a drop of it had touched them. When he expressed his surprise to the master that the mercy of God did not descend upon him also, the master replied that it would have done so if only he had remembered when they were at the fortress.[3]

[1] In the somewhat more detailed version of this story in the *Durrah*, he and his fellow-travellers were ambushed just three miles outside his native town to which he was returning from Seville (Cf. below p. 68). It is also related there that he remained with his captors for six months.

[2] al-Qaṣr al-Kabīr. Cf. *Archives Marocaines*, II, 2e, p. 19.

[3] This story is also told in the *Durrah* (see Introduction). In that version al-'Uryanī is ordered by God not to enter the fortress and it is Ibn 'Arabī himself who asks the master why the rain had not fallen also on him. Cf. Esad Ef. 1777, f. 93b.

Fez. Photo: *O. J. Watson*

The Great Mosque of Cordova. Photo: *O. J. Watson*

to face page 64

One day, while I was sitting with him, a man brought his son to the master. He greeted him and told his son to do the same. By this time our master had lost his sight. The man informed him that his son was one who carried the whole of the Qur'an in his memory. On hearing this the master's whole demeanour changed as a spiritual state came upon him.[1] Then he said to the man, 'It is the Eternal which carries the transient. Thus it is the Qur'an which both supports and preserves us and your son.' This incident is an example of his states of spiritual Presence.[2]

He was staunch in the religion of God and in all things blameless. Whenever I went to see him he would greet me with the words, 'Welcome to a filial son,[3] for all my children have betrayed me and spurned by blessings[4] except you who have always acknowledged and recognized them; God will not forget that.'

Once I enquired of him how his spiritual life had been in the early days. He told me that his family's food allowance for a year had been eight sack-loads of figs,[5] and that when he was in spiritual retreat his wife would shout at him and abuse him, telling him to stir himself and do something to support his family for the year. At this he would become confused and would pray, 'O my Lord, this business is beginning to come between You and me, for she persists in scolding me. Therefore, if You would have me continue in worship, relieve me of her attentions; if not tell me so.' One day God called him inwardly, saying, 'O Aḥmad, continue in your worship and rest assured that before this day is over I will bring you twenty loads of figs, enough to last you two and a half years.' He went on to tell me that before another hour had passed a man called at his house with a gift of a sack-load of figs. When this arrived God indicated to him

[1] See Introduction, p. 54.

[2] This is the absorption of the inner consciousness of the heart in the contemplation of God and its abstraction from the world of forms. Cf. al-Ḥujwīrī, *Kashf al-Maḥjūb* (E. J. W. Gibb Mem. XVII) 1911, pp. 248–51.

[3] The relationships here referred to are of a spiritual kind. The celebrated Fāṭimah (see below, p. 173) once told Ibn 'Arabī's mother that he was, spiritually, her father. Cf. *Futūḥāt*, II, 348.

[4] In as far as every true spiritual master is a channel of divine grace, his instruction and supervision, as indeed his mere presence might be said to impart essential benefits to one receptive enough. Cf. F. Shuon, 'The Nature and Function of the Spiritual Master', *Studies in Comparative Religion*, I, pp. 50–9.

[5] The author here explains that each load of figs weighed one hundred rotls, a rotl being approximately one pound in weight.

that this was the first of the twenty loads. In this way twenty loads had been deposited with him before the sun set. At this his wife was most grateful and his family well content.

The Shaikh was much given to meditation and in his spiritual states generally experienced great joy and hope.[1]

On my last visit to him, may God have mercy on his soul, I was with a company of my fellows. We entered his house to find him sitting and we greeted him. It happened that one of our company was intending to ask him a question on some matter or other, but as soon as we had entered, he raised his head to us and said, 'Let us all consider a point which I have previously put to you, O Abū Bakr (meaning me), for I have always wondered at the saying of Abū al-'Abbās b. al-'Arīf,[2] "That which never was passes away, while He Who ever is subsists." We all know that that which never was passes away and that He Who ever is subsists, so what does he mean by it?' None of the others in our company were prepared to answer him so he offered the question to me. As for me, though I was well able to deal with the question, I did not do so, being very restrained in speaking out. This the Shaikh knew and he did not repeat the question.

When he retired for sleep he did not remove his clothes and when he experienced Audition[3] he did not become disturbed, but when he heard the Qur'an being recited his restraint broke down and he became very agitated.[4] One day I was praying with him at the house of my friend Abū 'Abdallāh Muḥammad al-Khayyāṭ,[5] known as the starcher (*al-'Assād*), and his brother Abū al-'Abbās Aḥmad al-Ḥarīrī,[6] when the Imām[7] was reciting the chapter of the Qur'an entitled 'The Tiding'.[8] When he came to the place where God says, 'Have we not made the earth a

[1] The spiritual state (*ḥāl*) is the temporary action of a spiritual grace bestowed upon the Sufi in accordance with his condition and aspiration. Cf. Introduction, p. 54.

[2] This celebrated Spanish Sufi was the author of the *Maḥāsin al-majālis*, ed. Asin Palacios, Paris, 1933. He died in AD 1141.

[3] Audition as a general principle is the awakening of inner spiritual states through the inner force of some external sound. More specifically, it is listening to music or poetry in order to induce such states, as is practised by certain of the Sufi orders. Cf. Ḥujwīrī, *Kashf al-maḥjūb*, pp. 393 ff.

[4] Regarded as the Word of God, the Qur'ān must necessarily often evoke responses of this kind in properly receptive listeners.

[5] See below, p.91.

[6] See below, p. 95.

[7] The leader of the congregation in prayer.

[8] Qur'an, LXXVIII.

resting place and the mountains for supports. . . .'[1] I became abstracted from the *Imām* and his recitation and saw inwardly our Shaikh, Abū Ja'far, saying to me, 'The resting place is the world and the supports are the believers; the resting place is the community of the believers and the supports are the gnostics; the gnostics are the resting place and the prophets are the supports; the prophets are the resting place and the apostles are the supports; the apostles are the resting place and then what?'[2] He also uttered other spiritual truths, after which my attention returned once more to the reading of the *Imām* as he was reciting, '. . . and He speaks aright. That is the true day.'[3] After the prayer I asked him about what I had seen and found that his thoughts concerning the verse had been the same as I had heard him express in my vision.

One day a man rushed upon him, knife in hand, to kill him, at which the Shaikh calmly offered his neck to the man. The Shaikh's companions tried to seize the fellow, but the Shaikh told them to leave him alone to do what he had been urged to do. No sooner had he raised the knife to cut the Shaikh's throat than God caused the knife to twist about in the man's hand so that he took fright and threw the knife to the ground. Then he fell down at the Shaikh's feet full of remorse.

Were it not for the lack of space I would have related much more concerning this man, of his amazing aphorisms and the discussions we had on spiritual questions.

FROM 'AL-DURRAT AL-FĀKHIRAH'[4]

This Shaikh had turned to God while attending the sessions (*majlis*) of the Shaikh Abū 'Abdallāh b. al-Ḥawwāṣ whom I met and with whom I established a true companionship. I have omitted his Shaikh from this selection since he does not come within the category of persons considered in this work.

[1] *Loc. cit.*, v. 6.

[2] These meditations upon the Qur'anic verse express a hierarchical view of the universe. A prophet is one inspired by God to proclaim His messages and an apostle is the bringer of a new divine dispensation. Thus the apostle is, by implication, also a prophet, whereas a prophet is not necessarily an apostle. Cf. *Sagesse des prophètes*, by Ibn 'Arabī, trans. T. Burckhardt, Paris, 1955, p. 46.

[3] Qur'ān, LXXVIII, 38–9.

[4] Esad. Cf. 1777 f. 91б.

Al-'Uryanī was well known for his being engaged in Invocation whether he was awake or asleep;[1] I myself would often watch his tongue moving in Invocation while he was sleeping. His spiritual states were intense and the people of the locality were ill-disposed towards him, so much so that one of the leading members of the community persuaded them to expel him.[2] It was in this way that he came to us in Seville.

As a result of their action God sent to the people of that place one of the *Jinn*,[3] called Khalaf, who occupied the house of the above-mentioned leader and forced him out. This *Jinn* stayed in the house and called the people of the place to come to him, which they did. When they had come to the house they heard the voice of the *Jinn* asking one of their number if something had been taken from his house and whether he suspected anyone of taking it. Having answered in the affirmative to both questions the *Jinn* told him that he was wrong in his suspicions and that the name of the real culprit was so and so who was in love with his wife and had committed adultery with her. The *Jinn* then bade him go and see for himself and he found all that the *Jinn* had told him to be true. In this way the *Jinn* continued to expose their hidden evils and vices to them and their children until he drove them to despair. When they begged him to leave them alone he replied that he had been inflicted upon them by 'Abdallāh (al-'Uryanī). He remained with them for a period of six months, after which time they came to al-'Uryanī and begged him to return to the town, imploring him to forgive them for what they had done to him. The Shaik relented and returned to that place to relieve them of the *Jinn*. The affair became famous throughout Seville. . . .

One day when I was with him he asked for something to drink. One of his female disciples got up and brought him a jug in a copper stand with a lid of copper. When he saw it he said, 'I have no wish to drink what lies between two unlucky

[1] The constant practice of invocation (*dhikr*) of sacred names is a feature of all the major spiritual traditions. In the Christian tradition the 'Prayer of the Heart' of the Eastern Hesychasts is the most noteworthy example of this practice. Cf. T. Burckhardt, *An Introduction to Sufi Doctrine*, Lahore, 1959, pp. 124 ff.

[2] He came from 'Ulyā' which is now Loulé near Silves in the Algarve.

[3] The *Jinn* are beings of a subtle nature, whether well-disposed towards men or working against them. Cf. *Encyclopaedia of Islam*, art. *Djinn*.

things.'[1] I then brought him another jug. God made of everything his senses conveyed to him a means of teaching him some wisdom.

---

2 ABU YA'QUB YUSUF B. YAKHLAF AL-KUMI[2]

This Shaikh had been one of the companions of Abū Madyan[3] and had met many of the most prominent Sufis of this land. For a time he had lived in Egypt and had married in Alexandria.[4] Abū Ṭāhir al-Salafī[5] had wanted him to marry into his family. On one occasion he was offered the governorship of Fez, but he refused. He was one of those who are well established on the Way. Abū Madyan, who was the spokesman of our order and the one who revived it in the West, said of Abū Ya'qūb, that he was as a safe anchorage is to a ship.

He was much given to private devotions and always gave alms in secret. He honoured the poor and humbled the rich, ministering in person to the needs of the destitute. While I was in his charge he instructed me and looked after me most excellently.

My companion, 'Abdallāh Badr al-Ḥabashī,[6] knew him well and the Shaikh died at his house. He used to say of the Shaikh that he could, if he wished, raise the postulant from the lowest depth to the highest spiritual height in a moment. His powers of Concentration were considerable. He followed, for the most part

[1] The word for copper (*nuḥās*) comes from the root *naḥisa* which means to be unlucky or inauspicious. The two malefic planets, Mars and Saturn, are called in Arabic *Al-Naḥsān*.

[2] Cf. *Futūḥāt*, I, p. 251; III, p. 45.

[3] Shu'aib b. Ḥusain Abū Madyan (d. AD 1197–8) was perhaps the most renowned master of his day and was quite clearly a major influence on Ibn 'Arabī. His tomb near Tlemcen in Algeria is still the object of pilgrimage. J.J.J. Bargès, *Vie du célèbre Marabout Cidi Abou Medien*, Paris, 1884.

[4] The Sufis, unlike the mystics of some other traditions, were not necessarily celibate; indeed Ibn 'Arabī himself had two sons and a daughter.

[5] Born at Isfahan in Persia in AD 1082, and died at Alexandia in AD 1180.

[6] See below, pp. 119 and 158

the rule of the Malāmiyyah.[1] He was seldom to be seen without a frown on his face, but when he saw a poor man his face would light up with joy; I have even seen him take one of the poor into his lap and he himself frequently acted as servant to his followers.

I saw him in a dream on one occasion and his breast seemed to be cleft asunder and a light like that of the sun shone out from it. In the dream he called out to me to come to him. I came to him with some large white bowls which he proceeded to fill to the brim with milk. I drank the milk from the bowls as fast as he filled them.[2] Wonderful indeed is the spiritual grace I have received from him, as also from Abū Muḥammad al-Mawrūrī, whom I will mention later.[3]

At our first meeting, the first question he put to me, with all his concentration fixed upon me, was, 'What is the sin of him who passes in front of one praying, the enormity of which is such he would wish he had stood where he was for forty years?' I answered him correctly and he was pleased with me.[4]

When I would sit before him or before others of my Shaikhs, I would tremble like a leaf in the wind, my voice would become weak and my limbs would shake. Whenever he noticed this he would treat me kindly and seek to put me at my ease which only increased my awe and reverence for him.

This Shaikh had a great affection for me, but concealed it from me by showing more favour to others and displaying a distant manner towards me, commending what others had to say, but taking me to task at gatherings and sessions. He went so far in this that my fellows, while we were all together under his charge and in his service,[5] began to think little of my spiritual progress. However, praise be to God, I alone of the whole group

[1] This approach to following the Way of God stresses the awareness of and the discounting of the blame (*malāmah*) and disapproval of men in seeking the approval of God in accordance with the verse, 'They fear the blame of no man . . .' (Qur'ān, V, 54). Cf. Ḥujwīrī, *Kashf al-maḥjūb*, pp. 62–9, 183–4.

[2] Milk is often used as a symbol for knowledge.

[3] See below p. 101.

[4] Bukhārī, *Ṣalāt*, CI.

[5] As with spiritual aspirants of other traditions, those seeking to follow the Sufi Way would attend upon some noted spiritual master from whom they would receive guidance and instruction and later, if fitted, initiation. The postulants would, in return, minister to the master's external needs, which service in itself constituted an essential part of the preparation for the travelling of the Way. Cf. Ḥujwīrī, *Kashf al-maḥjūb*, pp. 334 ff.

achieved real success in my studies with him, which the Shaikh himself later admitted.

Another experience I had with this Shaikh is worthy of mention. Firstly, it must be explained that I had not at that time seen the *Epistle* of al-Qushairī[1] or any other master, being quite unaware that any of our Way had written anything, nor was I acquainted with the proper terminology of the Sufis.

One day the Shaikh mounted his horse and bade me and one of my companions follow him to Almonteber,[2] a mountain about three miles distant from Seville. Accordingly, when the city gate had been opened in the morning, I set out with my companion who had with him a copy of al-Qushairī's *Epistle*. We climbed the mountain and found the Shaikh at the top and his servant holding his horse. Then we entered the mosque at the top of the mountain and performed the ritual prayer.[3] When we had finished he turned his back on the *miḥrāb*[4] and gave me the *Epistle*, telling me to read from it. My awe of him was so great that I could not put two words together and the book fell from my hands. Then he told my companion to read it and expounded upon what was read until it was time for the late-afternoon prayer which we performed.[5] After the prayer the Shaikh suggested that we all return to the town. He mounted his horse and set off, while I ran alongside holding onto the stirrup: Along the way he talked to me of the virtues and miracles of Abū Madyan.[6] As for myself, I was so absorbed by what he was telling me, looking up at him all the time, that I was completely oblivious to my surroundings. Suddenly he looked at me and smiled and, spurring his horse, made me run the more quickly to keep up with him. Then he stopped and said to me, 'Look and see what you have left behind you!' When I looked back I saw that all the way was waist-high with thorn

[1] One of the most important and definitive works on Sufism from the pen of a Sufi, al-Qushairī (AD 986–1074). The *Risālah* was published in Cairo in four volumes (1290 AH).

[2] It is not certain which mountain is meant here.

[3] The daily ritual prayers are five in number and are performed at specified times of day in accordance with strict conditions. Each prayer consists of a certain number of *rak'āt* or cycles of movement and certain liturgical texts are recited in Arabic. Cf. *The Encyclopaedia of Islam*, art. *Ṣalāt*.

[4] A *miḥrāb* is the niche in the wall of a mosque which indicates the direction of Mecca (*qiblah*).

[5] See note 3 above.

[6] See above p. 69, no. 3.

bushes and that the whole ground was covered with thorns. Then he told me to look at my feet and my clothes. I looked and found not a single trace of the thorns. Then he said, 'This is the result of the spiritual grace engendered by our talking of Abū Madyan; so persevere on the Way, my boy, and you will surely find salvation.' Then he spurred his horse on and left me behind. I learnt much from him.

It was a characteristic peculiar to this Shaikh that when he prescribed spiritual exercises for the postulant to perform, he always performed them himself, even if there were two or three of them working on different exercises. This never seemed to weary him.

One day, when I was sitting with him after the late-afternoon prayer, he perceived that I was anxious to leave. When he enquired of me the reason for my unease I explained to him that I had four obligations to fulfil for certain people, that I had only so much time in which to do so and that if I stayed with him I would no longer be able to find the people concerned. At this he smiled and said, 'If you leave me now and go off, not one of your obligations will be discharged, so sit with me while I tell you of the spiritual states of Abū Madyan. As for your tasks I will ensure that they are carried out.' I sat with him and when the time came for the sunset prayer he said to me, 'Go home now and you will find that before you have prayed the sunset prayer all your obligations will have been fulfilled.'

So earnest was I in seeking his company that I used often to wish that he might be present with me in our house at night to deal with some problem or other. At such times I would see him before me, whereupon I would put questions to him and he would answer me. In the morning I would go and tell him what had happened. The same thing would also happen during the day when I was at home, if I wished it.

This Shaikh's virtues, powers and expertise were such as I cannot possibly enumerate here.[1]

This Shaikh of mine provided me with much instruction concerning the matter of spiritual Union,[2] expounded according

[1] I have omitted here some verses in which the author extols the virtues of his Shaikh.

[2] The Union here referred to concerns that stage in which the soul experiences its relationship with its Lord as a relationship between the lover and the beloved.

to the following sayings: 'I am the chief of the sons of Adam'; 'Adam and those that come after him are under my banner'; 'Direction is the half of livelihood'; 'When God loves His servant He tries him'; 'The heart of the Qur'an is the chapter "Yasin".'[1] None other in our land knew more than he on this matter and others which I cannot now remember, may God be pleased with him.[2]

---

3 SALIH AL-'ADAWI
the Berber

This man was a true gnostic,[3] continually with God in all he did and devoted to the recitation of God's Holy Book at all times of the day and night. He never had a house of his own and cared not at all for his health, being of those who seek to attain to the station of the seventy thousand who shall enter into Paradise without the Reckoning.[4]

Sometimes he would be told that the sun was well into its decline while he was still engaged in the first part of the prayer of the forenoon. When he prepared himself for prayer on very cold days, he would throw off his outer garments, leaving himself only a single shirt and trousers; despite this he would perspire during the prayer as if he were in a small cell. Also, during his prayer he would groan and mutter so that no one could understand what he was saying.

He stored nothing for the morrow and accepted nothing beyond his bare needs, whether for himself or for others. At night he frequented the Mosque of Abū 'Āmir al-Rutundalī, the reciter.[5] I myself kept company with him for a number of years during which time he addressed so few words to me that I could almost count them.

[1] Qur'ān, XXXVI.

[2] This collection of sayings would seem to be by way of allusions given to a favoured disciple, the inner meaning of which may only be arrived at by a proper esoteric exegesis (*ta'wīl*). Cf. T. Burckhardt, *An Introduction to Sufi Doctrine*, ch. VI. They are to be found in: (i) Da'ūd, *Sunna* 13, (ii) Tirmidhī, *Manāqib*, 1, (iii) not traced, (iv) Ḥanbal, 5, (v) Ḥanbal, *Fitan* 14.

[3] See Introduction, p. 54.

[4] Bukhārī, *Bad' al-khalq*, VIII.

[5] Cf. Ibn Abbār, *Takmilah*, ed. Codera, p. 427.

One year he was away from Seville around the time of the Great Festival.[1] A certain jurist, a reliable man, told me that he was attending the gathering at 'Arafāt[2] and that he had been informed of this by one who had seen him there.

He maintained a special connection with us and often directed his meditation to us from which we gained great spiritual benefit. Concerning myself he told me many things which, later on, proved completely correct.

He was attended in his illness by Abū 'Alī al-Shakkāz.[3] He remained thereafter in Seville for forty years until he died there. We ourselves washed his body for burial by night and carried him on our shoulders to his grave where we left him for the people to pray over and then bury. Since that time I have never seen his like. The manner of his life was like that of 'Uwais.[4]

FROM 'AL-DURRAT 'AL-FAKHIRAH'[5]

He spent forty years in the wilderness and forty in Seville.

One day I came to see him when he was performing the ritual ablution.[6] While performing this rite his colour would change from shame and fear. When he was asked about this he replied, 'How else should be the state of one who prepares himself, full of sin though he be, for converse with his Lord?' He performed his ablution meticulously, washing each part three times and each time making mention of God, as is proper.

When he had completed his ablution he looked up and saw me standing there. He was sitting on a bench preparing to wipe himself down, and he called me over to him. At that time I had just

[1] This Muslim festival which commemorates the sacrifice of his son by Abraham is celebrated on the tenth day of the month Dhū'l-Ḥijjah, the pilgrimage month. It is also called *'Id al-Aḍḥā*, the Festival of the Sacrifice.

[2] This forms part of the Pilgrimage rites. Cf. *Encyclopaedia of Islam*, art. *Hadjdj*.

[3] See below, p. 96.

[4] Uwais al-Qaranī, an ascetic, lived in the time of the Prophet, but never saw him. The Prophet, however, knew of him and described him to 'Umar and 'Alī, bidding them visit him to convey his greetings. After the Prophet's death they sought him out and asked for his blessing. He warned them to be ready for the Day of Resurrection. Later he died fighting for 'Alī at the battle of Ṣiffīn.

[5] Esad Ef. 1777, f. 80b.

[6] Ritual purity is necessary for the performance of the prayer rite. Cf. *Encyclopaedia of Islam*, art. *Wuḍū'*.

begun to follow the Way and had received certain intimations of a spiritual nature which I had told to no one. He said to me, 'O my son, when you have tasted the honey, taste no more of vinegar. God has opened the Way to you, so stand firm in it. How many sisters do you have?' I told him I had two sisters. He asked me whether they were both unmarried to which I replied that they were, but that the eldest was promised to the Amīr Abū al-'Alā' b. Ghazūn. Then he said to me, 'My son, know that this match is not to be, for both your father and this man you speak of will die and you will be left to look after your mother and sisters. Your family will try to persuade you to return to the world to care for your mother and sisters. Do not do as they ask nor heed their words, but recite to them God's words: "Bid your people pray and persevere in it. We do not ask you for sustenance, for it is We Who provide and for the righteous will be a good issue."[1] Do no more than this, for God has prepared a way of release for you. If you listen to them you will find yourself denied both in this world and in the Hereafter and left to make your own way.'

Before the end of the same year the Amīr died before his marriage with my sister could be consummated. Six years later my mother died. The Shaikh had also died. In due course my family came to me and took me to task for failing to earn a living for my dependants. Then my cousin came to me and with great kindness begged me to return to the world for the sake of the family. In reply I recited to him two verses which I had composed on the spur of the moment:

They bade me turn aside from the Way of God and I replied,
How can I leave the Way when the Friend has said,
After the morning light of the Reality, what is there but the
 dark night of error. Thus I cannot do what you ask of me.

However, the Prince of the Faithful[2] wanted me to enter his service. To this end he sent to me the late Chief Justice Ya'qūb Abū al-Qāsim b. Taqī. He had told the judge to meet with me alone and not to attempt to force my hand if I refused his suggestion. When he came and put the proposition to me, I refused, the Shaikh's words ringing in my ears. Then I met the

[1] Qur'ān, XX, 132.
[2] This must be Abū Ya'qub Yūsuf, the Almohad. AD 1163–84.

Prince and he enquired about my two sisters who were in need of protection. I told him of their situation. He then offered to find suitable husbands for them, to which I replied that I would look after the matter myself. On hearing this he told me that I was being too hasty and that he had a duty towards them. He then called his door-keeper and bade him, with some insistence, to inform him, by day or night, when my reply should come. Not long after I had left the Prince he sent a messenger after me to repeat his offer with respect to my two sisters.

I thanked the messenger, but left almost at once with my family and a paternal cousin for Fez. After a few days the Caliph asked Abū al-Qāsim b. Naḍīr about me. He told him that I had gone with my family to Fez. At this the Caliph repeated the saying, 'Glory be to God.' When we had settled in Fez I married off my two sisters and was thus relieved of their charge. Thereafter the Shaikh's spiritual grace returned to me and I came to Mecca. This is one of the instances of the Shaikh's spiritual graces.

When he died we washed his body by night secretly and carried him on our shoulders to the graveside where we left him. By morning the news of his death had spread far and wide. Before long there remained with the Prince of the Faithful no-one but his door-keeper. When he asked what was happening he was told about the Shaikh's death and also about what we had done and he realized what his men were doing among the people. Then the Prince went out and attended the burial, but was not accorded recognition by the people until he stopped looking upon them with contempt.

I was his companion for nearly thirteen years.

4 ABU 'ABDALLAH MUHAMMAD AL-SHARAFI[1] of Aljarafe

This Shaikh used to pray all the five prescribed prayers in the Friday Mosque of 'Udais in Seville. He made his living from the sale of opium, which he collected in the proper season and sold

[1] Cf. *Futūḥāt*, I, p. 206.

to people known for their uprightness whose money was good.

He used to stand so much in prayer that his feet would swell from it, and when he prayed the tears would fall down his face on to his beard like pearls. He occupied the same house for forty years without light or fire, devoting himself assiduously to worship.

One day he came upon me while I was looking at the local madman. I didn't notice him until he took me by the ear, pulled me away from the crowd and said, 'Is this the sort of thing you indulge in?' At his words I felt very ashamed and went off with him to the mosque.

He used to tell me of things before they occurred and they would always happen as he had said.

He would never pray twice in the same place in the mosque. Since none would dare openly to ask him to pray for them, whoever wished to benefit from his supplications would look to see where he would pray in the mosque and then go and pray beside him. When the Shaikh sat to make his supplications, the person desiring his help would make his own supplication aloud, to which the Shaikh would add the Amen; such was the power of his supplication.[1] Once I asked him to pray for me which he did, starting the supplication for me, 'Praise be to God.' He would always address me before I addressed him, for I held him in high esteem and derived great spiritual benefit from him.

With regard to his spiritual graces, I noticed that as his death approached he sent everyone away from him, saying that he wished to make a journey. He set off for his native village in Aljarafe, about six miles distant from Seville. After his arrival in that place he departed this life, may God have mercy upon him.

One day he saw a young boy with a basket of fennel on his head and the boy appeared to be very distressed. The Shaikh showed sympathy to the boy who asked for his supplication. By this time a crowd of people had gathered around them. When he asked the boy what distressed him he replied that his father had died, leaving several young children with no means

[1] Supplications (*du 'ā'*) are prayers said outside the canonical prayers, often immediately following them. Although they are regarded as a more personal form of prayer and may be said in a language other than Arabic, they usually take the form of Arabic prayers handed down from the Prophet, his Companions or some great Saint, which are considered to confer spiritual grace.

of support; his mother had told him to take the fennel she had and, if it were sufficient, to sell it for a day's supply of food. At this the Shaikh wept and, putting his hand into the basket, he took out a few grains. Then he said to the boy, 'This is good stuff, my boy; so go and tell your mother that your uncle from Aljarafe has taken some of it, thus putting himself in your debt. Then one of the merchants took the basket saying, 'The Shaikh has taken some of it, so it is full of his blessing.'[1] Then the merchant went off and paid the boy's mother seventy Mu'min dinars in the basket.[2] What the Shaikh did was intended as an act of mercy.

FROM 'AL-DURRAT AL-FAKHIRAH'[3]

He was always away from the country at the time of the Pilgrimage.[4] He was seen there by a group of people from Seville who were also performing the rite.

One day I was with him for the noon prayer at the Mosque of 'Udais, when he noticed a large company of people. When he asked me what they were about I told him that the judge had gathered them together to agree on the appointment of a new *muḥtasib*[5] to supervise their affairs; they had agreed that it should be al-Irnāq. When he heard this he smiled and said, 'After I have prayed the noon prayer they will find that someone they have not chosen has been set over them.' I asked who it might be and he replied that I would find out after the prayer. Then I prayed the prayer with him and when we had finished the judge announced that he had decided to appoint al-Ṭalabī to the post. Then he departed. The Shaikh said to me, 'You see, he dealt with them as an intelligent man deals with his wife; he

[1] An holy man is considered to imbue all he has contact with with his spiritual grace. This principle lies behind the devotion to relics in all traditions.

[2] These are the dinars struck by 'Abd al-Mu'min, founder of the Almohads, who ruled in Spain from AD 1145 to 1212.

[3] Esad Ef. 1777, f. 83a.

[4] The Pilgrimage (*ḥajj*) is one of the five fundamental institutions of Islam the performance of which is incumbent on every able Muslim once during his lifetime. The rites connected with the Pilgrimage are performed in and around Mecca. Cf. *Encyclopaedia of Islam*, art. *Hadjdj*.

[5] The *muḥtasib* was a local official who supervised a wide range of activities, with special regard to the adherence to proper behaviour in carrying them out. Cf. Op. cit., art. *Muḥtasib*..

consults with her, but does not necessarily act in accordance with her views.'

5 ABU YAHYA AL-SINHAJI[1]

He was an old blind man who was employed in the Zubaidi mosque until his death. We ourselves buried him at Almonteber[2] and spent the night by his grave. I associated with him and found him most earnest in his worship, a man well grounded in the spiritual disciplines and sciences. I always saw him sit in a very small chair.

He died among us at Seville and after his death we had evidence of his spiritual grace. The mountain on which we buried him was very high and never free from winds; on the day of his burial God calmed the winds. This the people regarded as auspicious and they came and spent the night at the grave, reciting the Qur'an. When the people had left the mountain the winds blew as furiously as ever. Before his death I was well known as an associate of his.[3] He used to be much given to wandering, especially near the coasts, in search of seclusion from men.[4]

6 ABU AL-HAJJAJ YUSUF AL-SHUBARBULI[5]

of Shubarbul

He was from Shubarbul, a village in the Aljarafe, about six miles from Seville. He spent most of his time in the wilderness. He was a companion of Abū 'Abdallāh al-Mujāhid[6] and earned

[1] Cf. *Futūḥāt,* I, p. 206.

[2] It has not been possible to identify this place.

[3] This story is also told in the *Futūḥāt,* I, p. 206.

[4] *Khalwah* or retreat from men and the world is an important feature of all traditional spirituality. Some of the Sufis practised it for the greater part of their lives, while others resorted to it only at certain times to restore that spiritual integrity which converse with the world inevitably impairs. Ibn 'Arabī himself wrote a treatise on the subject in which he gives instructions for intensive retreat: *Kitāb al-khalwah,* Aya Sofya, 1644.

[5] Cf. *Futūḥāt,* I, p. 206. Ibn Abbār, *Takmilah,* no. 2083.

[6] See below, p. 146.

his livelihood by the sweat of his brow. He entered on the Way before he had reached puberty and continued on it until he died. Ibn al-Mujāhid, the leader of our order in this country, showed him great respect when he came to visit him and said of him, 'Seek the supplication of Abū al-Ḥajjāj al-Shubarbulī.' It was Abū al-Ḥajjāj himself who related this to me.

He told me that he used to visit Ibn al-Mujāhid, our Shaikh, every Friday and that on one particular Friday he found him repairing a wall of his house which had fallen down, in order to provide shelter for his household. After he had greeted him Ibn al-Mujāhid said to him, 'O Abū al-Ḥajjāj, you have departed from your usual practice; today is Thursday.' To this Abū al-Ḥajjāj replied that it was Friday. He went on to tell me that Ibn al-Mujāhid, on hearing this, clapped his hands and cried, 'Woe is me, this is all because of the job I had to do; what on earth would happen if I had more to do?' He then grieved for the time he had lost for worship. Abū al-Ḥajjāj himself was weeping as he told me about it. Finally he said, 'Thus do the brethren grieve for any opportunity they have missed for practising the presence of God.'

Although Abū al-Ḥajjāj was among the most eminent among us, he continued to keep himself by the work of his own hands until he became too weak to do so and had to rely upon the support of pious donations.[1] When he grew old and became too infirm to move about he would weep and say to me,' My son, God has caused me to be sought after and visited by people and has thus exposed me to temptation; for who am I that I should deem myself worthy of all this? Would that I were in good health, for it is I would dearly like to visit people in their homes rather than that they should come and see me.'

He was indeed a mercy to the world. When the Sultan's men came to see him he would say to me, 'O my son, these men are God's assistants engaged in the affairs of the world; it is thus quite fitting that men should pray on their behalf that God may show forth his truth by their works and assist them.' He enjoyed the goodwill of the Sultan.

No matter how many people came to visit him he would put whatever food he had in front of them, leaving nothing aside for himself. One day, when a group of people were visiting him

[1] In other words the charitable gifts of the Faithful.

he had me bring down the provision basket for them. This I did, but found in it a mere handful of chick-peas. These he offered to them.

I myself have witnessed many evidences of his spiritual grace. He was one of those who could walk on water.

At his house in the village he had a well, the water from which he used to perform his ritual ablutions. We noticed that there was, next to the well, a high fruit-bearing olive tree with a stout trunk. One of our companions asked him why he had planted the tree in such a place, where it restricted access to the well. Then he looked up at us, his back being bowed with age, and replied that, although he had been brought up in the house he had not noticed the tree till then; such was his preoccupation with his inner state.

Whenever any of us entered his house we found him reading the Qur'an; he did not read any other book till the day he died.

This Shaikh had a black cat which used to sleep in his lap and which no one else was able to hold or fondle. He once told me that God had made the cat a means by which to recognize the Saints.[1] He explained that the apparent shyness in her was not an inborn trait, for God had made her very joyful in the company of God's Saints. I myself saw her rub her cheek against the legs of certain visitors and flee from others. One day our Shaikh, Abū Ja'far al-'Uryanī,[2] visited this Shaikh for the first time. When he arrived the cat happened to be in another room. However, before he had had the chance to seat himself, the cat came in and looked at him, whereupon she opened her paws, embraced him and rubbed her face in his beard. Then Abū al-Ḥajjāj rose to receive him and seated him, but said nothing. Afterwards he told me that he had never seen the cat behave in this way with anyone else and that she had continued in that way the whole time he was there.[3]

One day while I was with the Shaikh at a gathering, a man came to him who was afflicted with a terrible pain in his eyes, so that he cried out from the pain like a woman in labour. As he entered the house his screams disturbed those present, and the

[1] The Saints or Friends (*awliyā'*) are those rare men who enjoy a constant awareness of the divine presence. Cf. Ḥujwīrī, *Kashf al-maḥjūb*, pp. 210–41.

[2] See above, p. 63.

[3] Similar stories about the response of animals to certain psychic manifestations of spiritual power abound in religious literature.

Shaikh himself turned pale and began to tremble. Then the Shaikh raised his hand in blessing and laid it on his eyes, whereupon the pain ceased. Then the man lay prostrate like one dead. Finally he got up and left the house with the others, in perfect health.[1]

This Shaikh was accompanied at all times by one of the righteous, believing spirits.[2] One day I went to visit him with our Shaikh Abū Muḥammad al-Mawrūrī.[3] When we arrived I told him that I had brought one of the companions of Abū Madyan[4] to see him. At this he smiled and said, 'How amazing! Only yesterday Abū Madyan was with me.' It must be explained that Abū Madyan was at Bugia at the time, forty-five days journey distant. Thus, the visit of Abū Madyan to Abū al-Ḥajjāj had been of a subtle kind. The same sort of thing happened frequently between myself and the above-mentioned Abū Ya'qūb.[5] Indeed, Abū Madyan had long since ceased to travel in the ordinary way.

A great deal of what I remember of him cannot be recorded here, as is also the case with the others I have written about in this book. I have written of all of them only to show that our times are not completely lacking in Saintly men.[6]

FROM 'AL-DURRAT AL-FĀKHIRAH'[7]

One day I heard a voice reciting the Qur'an in the way he recited it. Concerning this I told him that it was one of the believing *Jinn*[8] who had asked me to let him keep company with me; he had pressed me in the matter and had bound me

[1] In as far as all spiritual power tends towards re-integration and re-alignment, the directing of such power to a psychic or physical disorder would tend to result in healing of some kind.

[2] The belief in formal beings of a subtle nature is held by most traditions. These beings may be good or evil. A lively awareness of the existence of such beings characterises much spiritual guidance. Cf. Qur'an, LXXII, 1–15.

[3] See below, p. 101. [4] See above, p. 69, n. 3. [5] See above, p. 69.

[6] Ibn 'Arabī here alludes to the impiety and spiritual laxity of his times, in which saintly men were generally still regarded with reverence by high and low alike. One cannot but wonder what he would think of our own times in which the saint and the contemplative are usually regarded as psychological misfits.

[7] Esad Ef. 1777, f. 79a.

[8] See above, p. 68, n. 3. In the earlier part of the *Rūh al-quds* he discusses the question more fully.

with an oath. I abided by it and allowed him to sit with me to study the Qur'an with me.

This Shaikh was like his own Shaikh, always answered when he made supplication and having the power to walk upon water.[1]

One night thieves broke into his house and took some things he had there. While all this was going on the Shaikh was on his prayer mat too absorbed in his devotions to notice their presence. When the thieves wanted to leave they could find no exit and the wall seemed to grow higher before their eyes. Then they returned the things and found the door. Then one of them stood by the door and the others went back for the things they had taken. No sooner had they done this than they could again not find a door. When they consulted their leader he assured them he had not left his place, but that he could no longer see the door. They repeated the operation several times without success. Then they finally realized what was happening, put the stolen goods back and left the house repentant. It was one of the thieves who told me this story.

I kept company with him for nearly ten years until he died.[2]

---

7 ABU 'ABDALLAH MUHAMMAD B. QASSUM[3]

This Shaikh used also to keep company with Ibn al-Mujāhid and studied with him until he died, after which he succeeded him and followed in his footsteps, proceeding even further than his master on the Way. He was a man of both knowledge and action, a Mālikite,[4] and a staunch upholder of learning and its excellence.

I used to attend upon him and studied with him as much as was necessary concerning ritual purity and prayer. I also heard his own works read.[5]

[1] See above, p. 77, n. 1. There follows an account of the incident of the well and the tree. When Ibn 'Arabī asks him about it he replies, 'As with excessive talking, excessive looking around is disapproved.'

[2] He died in 587/1191, when Ibn 'Arabī was twenty-six.

[3] Cf. *Futūḥāt*, I, p. 211; Ibn Abbar, *Takmilah*, no. 299.

[4] Ev-ery Sunnī Muslim is attached to one of the four schools of law (*madhāhib*). These are the schools of Mālik b. Anas, referred to above, and of Abū Ḥanīfah, Shāfi'ī and Ibn Ḥanbal. Cf. *Encyclopaedia of Islam*, art. *Sharī'a*.

[5] This is a method of witnessing to the genuineness of the work read.

His supplication at the end of every session was, 'O God, cause us to hear and see that which is good and may God bestow His forgiveness upon us and cause us to remain in it. May He also make our hearts to concentrate on righteousness and cause us to apply ourselves to that which is dear and pleasing to Him.' Then he would recite a portion from the final section of the chapter of the Qur'an entitled 'The Cow'.[1] We also used this prayer at the end of our own sessions.[2] One night, while I was in the Holy Sanctuary at Mecca I saw the Prophet in a dream in which a reader was reading the *Ṣaḥīḥ* of al-Bukhārī to him.[3] When the reader had finished, the Prophet prayed the same prayer; I therefore applied myself the more eagerly to this practice.

This Shaikh was most earnest and dedicated to self-discipline, being very precise in carrying out the acts of worship. In this connection he adhered to certain duties at fixed times to which he has kept to this day. He also carried with him a means of recording his deeds every day until nighfall which he would use in calling himself to account before retiring to bed. If he found good in himself he would praise God for it, and if he found bad he would say all the prayers necessary for forgiveness.

He used to make his living by making caps. One day he was sitting down to use his tools, his earnings being all spent, when he heard the door open and then close again. On going out to investigate he found no one, but discovered that someone had left six dinars for him, which he took. Then he took his shears and threw them down a well, saying, 'Both God and I are in charge of my livelihood, so why should I worry about what it will bring me? Your provision henceforth will seek for you and not you for it.'

I have already mentioned the way in which he used to apportion his day and night, but here are more details.

After he had prayed the morning prayer he would sit in

[1] The second and longest chapter of the Qur'an.

[2] The Sufi session or *majlis* is the gathering together of the disciples with their Shaikh or his representative to recite the litanies (*awrād*) of the order (*ṭarīqah*) and also to receive instruction from the Shaikh. Cf. *Encyclopaedia of Islam*, art. *Tarīqa*.

[3] Al-Bukhārī (AD 810–70) compiled one of the most important canonical collections of the Traditions of the Prophet. The *Saḥīh* was translated into French: El-Bokhari, *Les traditions islamiques*, Paris, 1903.

Invocation until the sun had risen, when he would pray two portions of the canonical prayer.[1] Then he would fetch his books and go out to the students who studied under him and stay with them until later in the morning, when he would return to his house to eat a little food if he wasn't fasting. Then he would pray the forenoon prayer and sleep a little. On rising from sleep he would perform the ritual ablution and then perform any task he had to do, otherwise he would sit in Invocation. When noon came he would open the mosque and call the people to prayer.[2] After this he would return to his house, perform the superrogatory prayers[3] and invoke the Name of God until the time of the noon prayer, when he would go to the mosque and perform the prayer, omitting the superrogatory prayers. While performing the prayer he would sway dizzily because of the ecstasy he experienced in uttering the Word of God.[4] When he had ended the prayer with the ritual greeting of Peace[5] he would leave the mosque and complete the assigned superrogatory prayers for noon. Then he would take the Qur'an upon his knees and, following the letters with his fingers and his eyes, he would intone it carefully and with feeling until he had completed the five parts.[6] When the time came for the late-afternoon prayer he would call to prayer, return to his house for the superrogatory prayers until the congregation had assembled, and then go and perform the prayer with them. He would then return to his house and sit in Invocation until the time of the sunset prayer, at which time he would call to the prayer and then perform it.

[1] See note above, p. 71. Each cycle or portion (*rak'ah*) of the prayer consists of the following principal parts: the intention (*niyah*); the saying of 'God is the most great' (*takbīr*); the standing (*qiyām*); the bowing (*rukū'*); the prostration (*sujūd*); the sitting (*jalsah*); the second prostration; and the greeting (*taslīm*). Cf. M. Lings, *A Sufi Saint of the Twentieth Century*, London, 1971, pp. 185–96.

[2] In Islam it is the human voice which summons the Faithful to prayer. This summons is called the *adhān*, the person who calls it being the *mu'adhdhin* (muezzin).

[3] The prayers for each time of day are divided into three main groups, each consisting of a certain number of prayer cycles or portions (see above). Firstly there are the obligatory portions (*farḍ*), secondly those established by Apostolic custom (*sunnah*) and lastly, those which are optional, but highly recommended (*nawāfil*).

[4] See above p. 66, n. 4.

[5] See above, n. 1.

[6] Since it is the custom to read the whole of the Qur'an in the month of the Fast (Ramaḍān), the Qur'an is divided into thirty parts (*juz'*), one for each day of the month. These parts are also subdivided each into two parts (*ḥizb*).

After that he would again return to his house. Sometime between the two night prayers, as darkness began to fall, he would light the mosque lamps and call to prayer, after which he returned to his house to say the superrogatory prayers. When the congregation had assembled he went and performed the prayer with them. After the prayer he would close the mosque. On returning to his house he would take a look at his record for the day, examining all his words and actions and all that he knew the Angel had recorded against him, so that he might act accordingly. He would then retire to bed and sleep. When a portion of the night had passed he would rise, perform the major ablution if he had lain with his wife,[1] and retire to his place of prayer, where he would recite the Qur'an, deriving great joy from it, whether on the transcendental plane, the plane of Paradise, the rational or the legal plane, according as the verses themselves indicated. In this way he would continue till morning.[2]

He received many spiritual sciences from God during these readings of the Qur'an which were not previously known to him. God Himself caused him to learn them from the Qur'an; for God has said, 'Fear God, for God it is Who teaches you.'[3]

When dawn broke he would go out to open the mosque, call to prayer, and light the lamps in the mosque. On returning to his house, he would pray the dawn prayer and sit in Invocation. When the light grew stronger he would go out again to pray with the people. This was the way in which our Shaikh spent his days and nights. He would only use salt on his food twice a week, on Mondays and Fridays. Both his spiritual state and station were high and his gnosis considerable. It is only seldom one meets such a man. I introduced to him my companion 'Abdallāh Badr al-Ḥabashī, and he prayed behind him.[4]

[1] After intercourse it is necessary to wash the whole body before performing the prayer. In the *Fuṣūṣ al-ḥikam* Ibn 'Arabī explains this as follows: 'There is no union (in this world) more intense than the conjugal act. Because of this, desire pervades all parts of the body and for this reason the Law prescribes total ablution. The purification must be as total as was the extinction of the man in the woman . . . because God is jealous of His servant.' (Ed. A. A. Afifi, Cairo, 1946, I, p. 217.)

[2] The Qur'an, regarded as the Word of God, necessarily embraces truth at many levels, which only those aided by divine grace are able to grasp. Cf. F. Schuon, *Understanding Islam*, London, 1963, ch. II.

[3] Qur'an, II, 282.

[4] See below, p. 158.

I kept company with him for nearly seventeen years.

When he prayed the midday prayer he would take the Qur'an and, placing it between his knees, would follow the letters with his finger and read it to himself until the time for the late-afternoon prayer. Thus he would continue the reading of the previous night. I asked him about it and he replied that he did this so that each of his members might acquire from his reading what was appropriate to it.[2]

---

8 ABU 'IMRAN MUSA B. 'IMRAN AL-MARTULI[3]
of Mertola

He once recited to me a poem of his addressed to himself:

> You are Ibn 'Imrān Mūsā the evil-doer,
> You are certainly not Ibn 'Imrān Mūsā who spoke with God.[4]

He imposed extreme spiritual discipline upon himself, having lived in the same house for sixty years without leaving it once. In his spiritual life he followed the way of al-Ḥārith b. Asad al-Muḥāsibī, accepting nothing from anyone and seeking nothing for himself or for others.[5]

I saw a vision concerning him which indicated that he would progress from the station he was in to a higher one.[6] When I told him of this he said, 'You have brought me glad tidings; may God also gladden your heart with the tidings of Paradise.' After a

[1] Esad Ef. 1777, f. 78a.

[2] This possibly refers to the teaching of the Qur'an that the various limbs and members will bear witness for or against their owners on the Last Day. Cf. Qur'an, XXIV, 24.

[3] Cf. *Futūḥāt*, II, pp. 6, 81, 177. He is mentioned frequently by his friend al-Balawī, *Kitab Alif Bā'* (1286), I, 23, 26, 153, 155, 389, 393, 410, 452–3, 489.

[4] This verse refers to Moses and his communication with God at the burning bush.

[5] Al-Muḥāsibī was among the greatest of the early Sufis, who, as his name suggests, laid great emphasis upon self-examination (*muḥāsabah*) and self-discipline (*mujāhadah*). He died in Baghdad in 243/AD 857.

[6] See Introduction, p. 54.

very short time he attained to the station indicated in my vision. The same day I went to see him. His face shone with joy when he saw me and he embraced me. Then I said to him, 'This is the interpretation of the vision I saw, so wish for me that God may grant fulfilment of His tidings for Paradise', to which he replied, 'If God wills it, it will be so.'

Before that month had passed God gave me tidings of Paradise by giving me a sign by which to establish the claim of the bringer of the tidings from God which encouraged me to believe the tidings when they came. Indeed, I was absolutely certain of the truth of these tidings and no more doubted that I was one of those destined for Paradise than that Muḥammad was a prophet, apart from the fact that I do not know for certain whether the fire will touch me or not. It is my sincere hope that, in His bounty, He will keep it from me, may God forgive us and you.[1]

This Shaikh was a man of great influence, deeply versed in gnosis and dedicated to noble dealings. Although he was, for the most part, in a state of great spiritual stress, he was always cheerful with his visitors.[2] We enjoyed many spiritual experiences with him and his inner power of Concentration (*himmah*) was fortified by God in preserving us from temptation and withdrawal from the Way, in which task he succeeded. With regard to myself, he attested to this himself. One day he said to me in the presence of my companion 'Abdallāh Badr al-Ḥabashi, 'I used to be anxious for you because of your tender years, the lack of any specific indications, the corruption of the times and the general deterioration I have observed in the brethren of the order. It was their corruption which drove me into seclusion, but God be praised for consoling me with you.'[3]

One day, when I went to see this Shaikh, he said to me, 'Be concerned with your own soul, my son.' I replied that when I had visited my Shaikh Aḥmad[4] he had told me to concern

[1] The servant ('*abd*) may never know fully the will of his Lord (*rabb*) for him.

[2] According to divine grace and the stage reached on the Way, the servant may experience the Self-revelation of God either in its aspect of Beauty which will bring him a state of spiritual Expansion (*basṭ*), or in its aspect of Rigour which will produce in him spiritual Stress (*qabḍ*). Cf. Ḥujwīrī, *Kashf al-maḥjūb*, pp. 374–6.

[3] I have omitted here some verses of no particular interest.

[4] This Shaikh is al-'Uryanī.

myself with God; so I asked him to which one of them I should give heed. He said, 'My son, I am concerned with my soul, while he is concerned with his Lord. Each of us guides you in accordance with his own spiritual state. May God bless Ibn 'Abbas and make me to reach his eminence.' Such was his impartiality.

He was always very open and frank with me, which only served to increase my respect for him. I surprised him in that I maintained this formal attitude towards him while he was so open with me. When he would return to the demeanour of servanthood I, for my part, would then be open with him. The reason for this is a wondrous mystery which you will understand, my friend, if you ponder upon it, if God will.[1]

FROM 'AL-DURRAT AL-FĀKHIRAH'[2]

He was Imam at the Mosque of Riḍā at Seville. He had served Ibn al-Mujāhid.[3] He composed a small collection of verses on the subject of asceticism which he would often read to me. He would leave his mosque only to attend the Friday prayer,[4] until increasing weakness of body prevented him from attending.

One day I went to see him and found with him the preacher Abū al-Qāsim b. Ghafīr,[5] a Traditionist who denied the miraculous powers of the Saints. As I entered I heard the Shaikh repudiating something he had said. The preacher was adducing against us two prohibited things which we ourselves had never committed and which we could not imagine any other of our number committing. I then asked the Shaikh, with whom I enjoyed a relationship of humble companionship, to leave the fellow to me. I said to him, 'O Abū al-Qāsim, you are a Traditionist are you not?' He replied that he was. Then I said, 'When the Apostle of God, upon whom be the peace and blessings of God, knew that his community would contain people of your

[1] According to the Sufis each 'time' (*waqt*) should evoke its own appropriate response in man. Whoever ignores or disregards what is appropriate to the moment, loses what it has to offer of truth. Cf. Ḥujwīrī, *Kashf al-maḥjūb*, pp. 367–70.

[2] Esad Ef. 1777, f. 108b.

[3] See below, p. 146.

[4] The Friday or congregational prayer would be performed in the main mosque of the city.

[5] Cf. *Futūḥāt*, II, p. 6.

kind, he denied the possibility of miraculous power in the case of those who simply obey God's commands. However, he did say one or two things which might cause you some confusion.' He then asked what they might be. I replied, 'Is it not related to us that the Apostle, the peace and blessing of God be upon him, said, "O my Lord, how many a dishevelled man clothed in rags and ignored by men might hold God Himself to an oath and He would keep it."[1] Did he not also say, "There are those servants of God who, were they to adjure God, He would fulfil their trust."[2] He further said, ". . . and among them are the absolved ones."[3] Do you accept these sayings?' When he had admitted them I said, 'Praise be to God Who did not restrict the Apostle to any particular kind of miracle, but granted him the possibility of an oath being adhered to by Him. He did not specify with what the oath should be concerned. Thus all possibilities are implied, so that were such a one to adjure God concerning walking on air or water, the travelling of great distances quickly, subsistence without food, the perception of what is in the souls and other things recounted of the righteous, God will fulfil that oath.' At this Abū la-Qāsim was very confused and fell silent. The Shaikh said to me, 'May God reward you with much good from His Saints!'

Once when I went to see him he was reciting the following lines:

> Cinnamon bark and a rough mat are often to be found in a house like mine.

The occasion for this verse was that God had granted some worldy favour to Abū al-'Abbas Aḥmād b. Muṭrif al-Qanjabārī, a righteous man, much given to spiritual endeavour and wandering, devoted to God. He came to our Shaikh and offered what he had received to him, but the Shaikh declined and composed the poem of which the above quotation is the first verse. He would never seek shelter in anyone's house nor accept provision from anyone. When someone came to him in distress he would commend his affair to God, which commendation always affected some relief for the person. He would never mention his own or anyone else's need out of shame before God. When

[1] Muslim, *Ḥudūd*, 18. [2] Bukhārī, *Ṣulḥ*, 8. [3] Not traced.

anyone else was in need he would sell some book from his valuable collection to feed that person from the proceeds of the sale. On one occasion when I visited him his collection of books had diminished greatly. When I commented on this he said that they were nothing but the cast-off remnants of his life. When they had all been sold he died, may God have mercy upon him. He died at Seville while I was here in the East.[1]

---

9 ABU 'ABDULLAH MUHAMMAD AL-KHAYYAT
the Tailor
and
10 ABU AL-'ABBAS AHMAD AL-JARRAR
the Potter

They were two brothers from Seville with whom I kept company in that place until the year 590/1194, when they set out to perform the Pilgrimage at Mecca. This was the year in which I visited you.[2]

After they had arrived in Mecca, Ahmad stayed there for a year, after which he went to Egypt and joined the Malāmiyyah.[3] Muḥammad, on the other hand, stayed in Mecca for five years and then joined his brother in Egypt in the same year that I left you, that is in the year 598/1201–2. I found them when I came to Egypt and stayed with them, during which time Abū 'Abdallāh was ill. While I was there I fasted the month of Ramaḍān with them.[4]

[1] That is some time after 598/1201. He was alive in 603/1206, according to al-Balawī, *K. Alif Bā'*, I, p. 153.

[2] Ibn 'Arabī visited Abū Muḥammad al-Mahdawī at Tunis. See Introduction, p. 27.

[3] See above, p. 70, n. 1.

[4] It is the duty of every Muslim to fast during the thirty days of the month of Ramaḍān from dawn until sunset. In addition it is usual to increase one's devotions and to read the whole of the Qur'an. It used to be common for the men of a Muslim community to spend most of the last ten days of the month in the mosques engaged in devotions (*i'tikāf*). Cf. Ḥujwīrī, *Kashf al-maḥjūb*, pp. 320–4. His visit to them was in 603/1206 (see above, p. 39).

Abū 'Abdallāh came to the Way long before his brother. He was a most filial son and attended to the needs of his mother till she died. So much was he dominated by the fear of God that the beating of his heart during prayer could be heard from a distance.[1] He wept much and kept long periods of silence, being always sad and pensive and prone to sighing.[2] I have never seen anyone more humble, always having his head bowed and his eyes cast to the ground. He mixed with no one. He was a man free from hypocrisy, strong in counsel, staunch in faith, blameless and patient although afflicted by poverty and misfortune. He was also a man of great spiritual influence and power and when I was young and studying the Qur'an with him I was very fond of him, he being one of our neighbours. Whenever he entered a mosque all who saw him showed him respect. He was never the first to speak and only answered when it was really necessary. He held firmly to the Faith and when I came to the Way I wished most to be like him and his brother.[3] I attached myself to him and derived great benefit from his conduct and example. He was also much pleased with me. He endured all hurt while refraining from inflicting it himself. His visions were true and he enjoyed much converse with his Lord. His nights were spent in prayer and his days in fasting. He was never idle and applied himself assiduously to learning.

Four of us, he and his brother, a companion and myself, used to gather together, all sharing equally in the spiritual insights granted to us on those occasions. I never knew better days than those.

Now follows an account of an incident indicative of his spiritual Concentration. Our house was some distance from his and it happened one night that, as the nightfall prayer was being called, I felt a strong urge both to be with him and also to go

[1] One of the requirements of true worship in Islam is a proper awareness of the directness of one's communication with God and a keen sense of His immediate presence inculcating a reverential awe and sense of majesty (*jalāl*). There are many accounts of the effects of prayer among the great Sufis. In his *Kashf*, Ḥujwīrī relates the story of a Sufi who was so absorbed in his prayer that he felt nothing when his leg was amputated (p. 304).

[2] The weeping of contrition or intense realization is often the outward sign of an inner melting of the heart's hardness in the flame of divine love. Cf. Qur'an, XIX, 58, also *Early Fathers from the Philokalia*, Kadloubovsky and Palmer, London, 1954.

[3] The text has *ukht* (sister), but his brother is more likely.

home, not knowing which course to take. Having chosen the first, I made for his house where I found him standing in the middle of the room facing towards Mecca. His brother was performing the superrogatory prayers. When I greeted him he smiled and said, 'What kept you? My heart was concentrated on you because you have on you something I need.' In fact, I had five dirhams in my pocket which I handed over to him. He explained that a medicant named 'Alī al-Salawī had called and that he had had nothing to give him. Then I returned home.

He used to attend in person to the needs of the poor, benefiting them with food and clothing. He was indeed a most kindly and sympathetic man, treating the young with mercy and the old with respect. To every man he gave his due and many were indebted to him, his only debt being to God. After this manner have I always found him, may God admit us both into His forgiveness.

As for his brother Abū al-'Abbās Aḥmad, what a man he was! A man replete with the virtues, avoiding all vices, one who knew God and was devoted to him, utterly trustworthy. He was of those who received divine communication 'from behind a veil',[1] Mighty in his contemplation, pleasing in company, helpful in all things and gentle, tolerant, agreeable to all which was pleasing to God, but firmly opposed to all not pleasing to Him. He invoked the Name and was ennobled by it and his name was on every tongue. Although he might sometimes seem absentminded, he could be as swift as one fleeing an avenger. He submitted himself to the authority of the mysteries and was a man much given to contemplation.

Whenever we were considering some point or other he would become inwardly absent from us, after which he would expound some aspect of the problem to us. He still acts in this way today.

He served only his brother through whose spiritual grace he enjoyed many spiritual benefits.

He met our Shaikh al-'Uryanī and Abū Muḥammad b. Junaid as also many other of our companions.[2] He would have liked to have accompanied us to Mecca had it not been for his

[1] 'It is not for a mortal that God should speak to him, except by revelation or from behind a veil or by sending an apostle. . . .' (Qur'an, XLII, 51).

[2] For al-'Uryanī, see above, p. 63.

brother's illness; indeed, had he been in good health we would all have travelled there together.

At about that time plague and famine were ravishing the people of Egypt.[1] One day this Shaikh of ours was walking along the street and saw young babies dying of starvation. At this sight he said, 'O Lord, what may all this mean?' Then he became lost to himself in contemplation, during which a voice said to him, 'O my servant, have I caused you loss in anything?' He said, 'No, indeed.' The voice continued, 'Do not interfere, for the children you see before you are the offspring of sin. These are a people who have made light of my statutes, so I have imposed the strictures of My Law upon them. Thus do I deal with those who make light of My statutes. Do not concern yourself with them.' When he came to himself again he found himself no longer distressed by what he saw. This Shaikh enjoyed many such discourses.

As regards preferring others to themselves, I have found none to better them in this respect, my God include me with them in His forgiveness and not separate us.

FROM 'AL-DURRAT AL-FĀKHIRAH'[2]

Abū 'Abdallāh Muḥammad al-Khayyāṭ

I had an empty jug in my house and one day I was preparing a gruel for the brethren, but had no honey or butter in the house to put into it. I then took the empty jug to him. He took it, held it in his hands and said over it, 'Eat in the name of God!' Then he proceeded to pour butter and honey from it on to the gruel.

One day when we were at the house of one of our our brethren he bought for us sweet pancakes and honey which we set about eating. When the honey had run out the owners of the house bade us be patient until some more could be bought. However, the Shaikh told us to dip our morsels once more into the dish and we would find what we were after. We did this and when we raised the morsels to our mouths they were dripping with honey. Then one of our number expressed a wish to see the honey. He then told us to clasp our hands together. As we did so

[1] Ibn al-Athīr, *Chronicon*, ed. Tornberg, XII, p. 112.
[2] Esad. Ef. 1777 f. 84a. El 85b.

I saw honey oozing from the edges of the dish until it was filled. Then we began to eat again and there was more than enough for all.

Abū al-'Abbās Aḥmad

He also died in Egypt. He used to be *Imām* at the Mosque of the Candles. He was known in Egypt as Aḥmad al-Ḥarīrī. He was firm and resolute in the religion of God as if he could see the Unseen with his own eyes.

---

11 ABU 'ABDALLAH B. JUMHUR MUHAMMAD

This man was a contemporary of Abū 'Alī al-Shakkāz[1] and the above-mentioned Abū 'Abdallāh al-Khayyāṭ,[2] one much given to worship. He had studied the Qur'an and the grammar of the Arabic language, but not prosody. It was told by Abū al-Ḥasan al-'Uthmānī that once, when he was young, he was reading the Qur'an to his Shaikh, when the sound of a tambourine could be heard, whereupon the Shaikh put his fingers into his ears and sat in silence. After a while he enquired whether the noise had stopped. On being told that it had not, he got up with his fingers still in his ears and retired to his quarters, summoning Abū al-Ḥasan to follow him so that he might complete the part he had begun to read to him.

Whenever he heard the voice of a beggar or of one reciting the Qur'an for the same purpose, he would stop up his ears. He was one of the 'bowing and prostrating ones' until he was taken from this life.[3] He was stout of heart, but weak of body, pale in colour and very hard on himself. When someone suggested to him that he be more gentle with his soul, he replied that it was in order to merit the compassion of God that he so exerted himself. During the hours of night he would stand and recite passages from the Qur'an until he collapsed from exhaustion. Only then would he lie down to sleep, saying to himself as he did so, 'O my cheek, since you cushion yourself so softly now, you will lie on hard rock after death.' At this he would leap up

[1] See below, p. 96. [2] See above p. 91. [3] Qur'an, IX, 112.

again, as if bitten by some snake and stay on his prayer carpet until morning.

He died while I was in the service of Abū Ya'qūb al-Kūmī.[1] As he was being lowered into his grave I saw an amazing thing: God had caused a large rock to be in the grave with him. Someone seeing this called attention to it, whereupon the person who was lowering his body into the grave took the rock and placed it under his cheek. Thus did God fulfil what he had said to himself before going to sleep.

An ascetic and a gnostic who secluded himself from men, he held closely to God and sought Union with Him, loving all those devoted to God and His Book. God took him from this life in his prime and at the peak of his spiritual endeavour. He would often say to his soul, 'Our efforts together will not be done until I die.' His devotion to the worship of God was unexcelled.

FROM 'AL-DURRAT AL-FĀKHIRAH'[2]

He grew up from childhood in the worship of God. He was learned in jurisprudence, the recitation of the Qur'an and the Arabic language. Whenever he went out on a journey with others he would insist that he was their leader and that they must obey him, to which they always agreed. His only purpose in this was to take their burdens upon his own back and thus relieve them.

---

12 ABU 'ALI HASAN AL-SHAKKAZ the Tanner

He was one of our group in Seville and died in that city, being one of those who served our Shaikh al-'Adawī[3] until he died.

This man was very prone to weeping and tears were seldom absent from his eyes. He used to keep company with an uncle of mine on my father's side who was one of the élite of the Folk of God.[4]

[1] See above, p. 69. [2] Esad. Ef. 1777, f. 89a. [3] See above, p. 73.

[4] This uncle is the subject of the following sketch. The Sufis often refer to themselves as the Folk (*qawm*) of God.

One night while I was at his house, he put down a new mat to pray on and, as he prayed, tears fell upon the mat. On the second day he took the mat away from that place, and the spot where his tears had fallen had begun to rot. I kept company with him from the time I entered the order till the day he died.

He was very attached to the married state and could not do without it. Our Shaikh al-Shubarbulī wanted to arrange a marriage between him and a niece of his.[1] One day Umm al-Zahrā' came to him and told him of the Shaikh's wish. The day was a Sunday. When he heard the news he bowed his head for a time, as if engaged in secret conversation. Then he got up and said, 'Of all men I would dearly like to be related to the Shaikh al-Shubarbulī, but I have already married and after five days I will produce my bride.' When he was asked to whose daughter he had become married, he replied, 'You will soon see!' Having returned to his house he retired to his bed for five days and died.

He would take the most bitter-tasting plants and feed them to you as if they were sweetmeats. He was possessed of many spiritual graces and I benefited much from my association with him. His method was that enunciated in the Forty Traditions of al-Suhailī.[2] He was a man of great courage and lived by his own labours. After his death his brother saw him in a vision and asked of him how God had treated him, to which he replied, 'Every day he gives me work enough for eight days.'

He was always fasting and often followed the practice of day-and-night fasting (*wiṣāl*).[3] He prayed much and avoided the company of all save his own kind. He was endowed with a great sense of humour for things spoken in a truthful spirit, but he hated falsehood and could not tolerate liars.

One day he went to the quarter of the Banū Ṣāliḥ to soak some skins in the river and then to stretch them out in the sun. As he was doing this a woman of Seville passed by. The Sevillians and their womenfolk are a witty and graceful people. She called her companion over to her and suggested to her that they enjoy a joke at the fellow's expense, since he was a tanner. It must be explained that among us the word *shakkāz* means one

[1] See above, p. 79.
[2] 'Abd al-Raḥmān al-Suhailī died near Malaga 581/1185.
[3] Cf. Bukhārī, *Ṣawm*, 20.

who is engaged in the bleaching and softening of skins and that the people of the locality use the word as a nickname for men who want nothing to do with women, in other words men who are soft-limbed like the skins they work with. The woman came and stood by him, but he was absorbed in Invocation which he performed tirelessly. She said, 'Peace be upon you, brother.' He returned the greeting and immediately went back to his Invocation. Then she asked him what he did for a living. He told her to leave him alone, knowing very well the object of her question. Then she said, 'You are not going to get away as easily as that.' Then he smiled and said, 'I soak what is dry, soften what is stiff and pluck what is hairy,' (thus avoiding the use of the word *shakkāz*). Thereupon she laughed and said, 'We wanted to catch him out, but he was outwitted us instead.'

He was a man of great spiritual influence, sound of heart, who never bore anyone a grudge. He was blissfully unaware of the ways of men and could not imagine how anyone could disobey God.

FROM 'AL-DURRAT AL-FĀKHIRAH'[1]

He never uttered the word 'I', nor did I ever hear him utter it. Because of an uncle of mine would often stay with us during my period of ignorance before coming to the order.

(Concerning the proposed marriage the version in the *Durrah* is somewhat different.)

We had sought a lady's hand for him in marriage and had resolved to see it through. I became ill, however, and when he came to visit me I spoke with him on the matter. He said, 'My brother, I am already married and on Thursday I will enter my bridal home.' This was on Saturday. Then he left me. Sometime after Umm al-Zahrā' came to see me, a woman dedicated to the Way of God. I mentioned to her what was afoot. When she had left me she went to him and discovered that almost as soon as he had left me he had fallen ill. When she spoke to him on the matter of the marriage, he said, 'O Fāṭimah, after five days I will enter my bridal chamber, as I told my brother Ibn al-'Arabī.' She asked, 'With whom will you marry, and how is it that you have a secret from us?' He replied, 'My sister, you will know on Thursday.' On Thursday he died, was buried and

[1] Esad Ef. 1777, f. 90a.

entered heaven, if God wills, a bridegroom on the night of Friday.

---

13 ABU MUHAMMAD 'ABDALLAH B. MUHAMMAD B. AL-'ARABI[1]

This Shaikh was my uncle on my father's side who came to the Way late in life through the agency of a young boy who knew nothing of the Way himself. He was in his eighties at the time. He persevered in self-discipline and seclusion from men by the coasts until he had achieved excellence on the Way. Every day he would read the Qur'an, a half of which reading he would dedicate to the boy who had been the cause of his coming to the Way.

While sitting in his house, he would often say, 'The dawn has come.' I once asked him how he knew this, seeing that he was sitting indoors, to which he replied, 'My son, God sends forth a wind from beneath the Throne, which blows in Paradise and which at dawn blows from Paradise, so that every true believer feels it every day.'

This uncle of mine suffered from a severe hernia which hung in front of him like a pillow. He had a wayward son who had caused him much bitterness. He called down God's curse upon him and he became ill. Then he prayed to God that he bring the son to judgement and then he himself would be ready to die. Accordingly, the son died before him and when they buried him he said, 'Praise be to God, I will survive this son of mine by fourty-four days, after which I will follow him.' He did indeed live as long as he said and then died.

On the night of his death we sat with him after the night prayer as he lay with his face towards Mecca, resting, since his hernia had become very large. After a while he told us all to go to our beds. In the early morning I got up, to find that he had passed away unnoticed. When we looked for the hernia we found nothing. It was then suggested that the swelling may have been due to a gas in which case the distended skin would still show. However, his skin was quite normal, like that of any

[1] Cf. *Futūḥāt*, I, p. 185.

normal person. I was astonished that God had caused it to disappear. During his life he often told us of miracles.

It was three years from the time he entered upon the Way to the day of his death, which was before I myself had started on the Way.

FROM 'AL-DURRAT AL-FĀKHIRAH'[1]

There was a shop near his house which belonged to a man who sold fresh herbs and drugs. My uncle often used to go and sit with this man in his shop. One day a handsome young boy who bore the marks of worship, came up to him, thinking him to be the owner of the shop, and asked him for some white nigella.[2] My uncle said (in a jocular tone), 'And what might that be?' The boy explained that he had been suffering from a certain complaint and that a woman had told him to use some white nigella. Then my uncle said, 'When I saw how ignorant you are, I laughed at you, because nigella is not white.' Then the boy said, 'O uncle, my ignorance in this matter will do me no harm in the sight of God, while your heedlessness of God will do you much harm, seeing that you persist in your opposition to Him despite your advanced years.' My uncle took this warning to heart and served the boy, becoming converted to the Way at his hands.

He lived three years after coming to the Way. During this time he attained to high spiritual degrees and came close to the mercy of God. He spent much time behind closed doors in his room of retreat.

He had a wayward son whose behaviour had become so troublesome to my father, that he wanted to have him banished from the land.[3] When my uncle heard of this he called me to him and said, 'My boy, go and tell my brother to leave my son alone, for he will die soon and we will be relieved of him. I will survive him by forty-two days and then join him in death; so your father will be relieved of us both.' It happened just as he had said.

[1] Esad Ef. 1777, f. 90b.
[2] A black aromatic seed not unlike all-spice.
[3] Ibn 'Arabī's father was in government service. Cf. below, p. 114.

14 ABU MUHAMMAD 'ABDALLAH, SON OF THE TEACHER, AL-MAWRURI[1]

of Moron

This man had served Abū Madyan[2] who used to call him the 'pious pilgrim'. He had performed the Pilgrimage with 'Abd al-Razzāq[3] and, while in Mecca, had kept company with Abū 'Abdallāh b. Ḥasan[4] The latter had offered his daughter to him in marriage as a mark of affection, but Abū Muḥammad had refused because he feared that he would be unable to fulfil all his obligations towards her.

Abū Madyan liked this man very much and said to him one day, 'I am weary of calling the people to God and finding no response, so I would like you to accompany me to some mountain cave, so that you may be with me till I die.' Telling this himself, Abū Muḥammad said, 'I rejoiced at his words and knew that I was certain of a place with God. During that night I saw in a dream that the Shaikh Abū Madyan when he preached to the people was like the sun, and that when he fell silent he was like the moon. Early next morning, when I related the dream to him, he smiled and said, "My son, praise be to God, for I would very much like to be like the sun which banishes all darkness and relieves all anxieties." '

This 'Abdallāh had great spiritual power and veracity. Once, as he was setting off on a journey from Abū Madyan's place at Bugia to Spain to see his mother, the Shaikh Abū Madyan asked him to convey his greetings to a certain Abū 'Abdallāh, an aged Shaikh known as al-Ghazzāl (the spinner) who lived in Almeria and who had been a companion of Ibn al-'Arīf[5] and a contemporary of Abū Madyan, Abū al-Rabī' al-Kafīf of Egypt, 'Abd al-Raḥīm of Qanā and Abū Najā of Jazīrat al-Dhahab.[6]

[1] Cf. *Futūḥāt*, IV, p. 76. It was to this Shaikh that Ibn 'Arabī dedicated his early work *Al-Tadbīrāt al-ilāhiyyah*, ed. H. S. Nyberg, in *Kleinere Schriften des Ibn al-Arabi*, Leyden, 1919.

[2] See above, p. 69, n. 3.

[3] A jurist and one of Abū Madyan's Tunisian disciples.

[4] Ibn Abbar, *Takmilah*, no. 728.

[5] See above, p. 66, n. 2.

[6] No information is available on these men.

When our Shaikh arrived in Almeria he went in search of the Shaikh Abū 'Abdallāh. Coming to his house he found the Shaikh's disciples sitting about in front of the house. He asked them to inform their Shaikh of his arrival. For their part they merely told him that their Shaikh was sleeping at that hour and did nothing to make him welcome. It grieved him that they were so insensitive as not to recognize him and said, 'If I have come on God's business, God will waken him now.' No sooner had he spoken than the door opened and there was the Shaikh, rubbing the sleep from his eyes and asking about the arrival of a visitor. Then he greeted him and honoured him with a fitting welcome.

Abū Muḥammad's spiritual state was usually one of Expansion, while Abū 'Abdallah's companions were in a state of Contraction. Therefore, as he was bidding them farewell, the Shaikh's companions said, 'O Abū Muḥammad, if only your Expansion were a little less!' He asked them what they meant by Expansion and they said, 'Mercy'. Then he asked them what they meant by Contraction and they said, 'Punishment'. Then he said, 'O God, remove me not from Your mercy to Your Punishment.' At this they all felt very ashamed.[1]

When he came to Granada he stayed with the Shaikh Abū Marwān whom he had known when they were together with Abū Madyan. Abū Marwān had personally witnessed a cure effected by Abū Madyan's companions on one of their number. This he had related to his companions in Granada. Therefore, when Abū Muḥammad arrived the people gathered in the house to see him and a table was laid out with dishes of curdled milk and honey. The host's son, however, had gone out early that morning to an outlying village and it grieved the company that he was not present to partake of the food with them.

After he and the rest of those present had eaten their fill, Abū Muḥammad said, 'If you like, I will eat the food for him here and he will feel sated wherever he is.' When they heard this they expressed doubts as to the possibility of such a thing, so Abū Marwān urged him to go ahead and perform what he had promised. After invoking God's Name, he began to eat as if he had had nothing at all. When he had finished he said, 'Our absent friend is now so sated that, were he to eat any more, he would

[1] See above, p. 88, n. 2.

die.' The people were amazed at this and resolved not to leave the house until the man for whom he had eaten should return.

In the late evening he returned and, after the people had made him welcome, they remarked on the fact that he still had with him the provisions he had taken with him that morning. Then the man explained: 'My brothers, a strange thing happened to me today. When I arrived at the village and sat down, I suddenly had the sensation of curdled milk and honey being poured down my throat and settling in my stomach until I was so full I would have died had I had any more of it. I am still full and belching even now.' The people were amazed and rejoiced that they had seen such a man.

He himself told me how it had happened. I was also told about it by the person who had been sated in this way, while I was at the house of 'Abdallāh al-Shakkāz al-Bāghī[1] with my companion 'Abdallāh Badr al-Ḥabashī[2] and a group of people. Al-Ḥabashī said regretfully, 'For myself, I have not met one like this 'Abdallāh al-Mawrūrī.'

One night God gave me a vision of the spiritual stations and took me through them till I came to the station of Reliance where I saw our Shaikh 'Abdallāh al-Mawrūrī.[3] He was at the centre of the station while the station itself revolved round him like the wheel round its hub, he being motionless.[4] Later I wrote to him about the vision. I used to spend much time with him and I gained much benefit from him.

He had a most beautiful wife, more handsome and stronger than he.

On one occasion he was with Shams, Mother of the Poor, at Marchena, the day being a Wednesday.[5] The old lady said, 'I would like Abū al-Ḥasan b. Qaiṭūn to come and see us tomorrow; so write and tell him to come!' Abū al-Ḥasan was at the time in Carmona, twenty-one miles away, where he taught the Qur'an to young boys. On Thursdays and Fridays he was free from work.

Then al-Mawrūrī said to the old lady, 'This is the way ordinary men would go about summoning him.' She said, 'What shall we do then?' He said, 'I will bring him to you by the power of my spiritual Concentration', at which she bade him do so. Then he said, 'At this very moment I have turned his thoughts to

[1] He is the subject of the next sketch.
[2] See below, p. 158.
[3] See Introduction, p. 54.
[4] *Futūḥāt*, IV, p. 76.
[5] See below, p. 142.

visiting us tomorrow, if God wills.' The next morning she said to him, 'You see, he has not come!' He explained that he had forgotten about him for a while, but that he would remedy the situation immediately. Then he directed his power once more upon the man. Shortly before noon, to everyone's astonishment, the man arrived despite al-Mawrūrī's forgetfulness.[1]

Then al-Mawrūrī told the people to ask the man what had delayed his arrival, how it had occurred to him to come and at what time he had decided to do so. The man told them that, on the previous day in the late afternoon, he had heard an inner voice telling him to go and visit the old lady in Marchena, whereupon he had told his boys not to attend the next day. He went on to say that the next morning his intention to make the visit had left him, which was the same time al-Mawrūrī had forgotten about him. Then the people urged him to go on with his story. He told them that he had gone to the school and the boys had arrived and taken out their slates, when he felt his heart under great stress and heard a voice telling him to go to Marchena. Then he had told his pupils to return to their homes. When he had finished his story he was told what had taken place at Marchena concerning him and he was astonished.

After this he held al-Mawrūrī in great respect and was so impressed that he travelled to Almeria to visit the Shaikh Abū 'Abdallāh al-Ghazzāl,[2] a companion of Ibn al-'Arīf[3] and a contemporary of Abū al-Rabī' al-Kafīf, Abū al-Najā and 'Abd al-Raḥīm.[4] He met with him there and gained much benefit from him, after which he returned to Carmona. After this time he continued to serve the brethren, provide them with hospitality and show them respect, which I liked in him.

However, I later saw this same man, when he came to Seville, attending upon the jurists and keeping company with those devoted to the things of this world. He took up the study of jurisprudence and theology. He stayed on in Seville to teach the Qur'an, but the company he was now keeping encouraged him to deny the spiritual attainments of the brethren and to reject them.[5]

[1] See above, p. 63, n. 4.
[2] See above, p. 101.
[3] See above, p. 66.
[4] See above, p. 101, n. 6.
[5] The following passage, which is a discussion of the evil motives of those who deny the Way, is added by Ibn 'Arabī in the margin of the manuscript.

God forbid, my brother, that you should think that I blame the jurists for being jurists or for their practice or jurisprudence, for such an attitude is not permissible for a Muslim and the nobility of the Law is beyond question. However, I do censure those jurists who, harbouring merely worldly aims, cynically study the Law with the sole object of acquiring fame, of putting themselves in the public eye, and who indulge in constant hair-splitting and useless controversy. It is such men who seek to refute the claims of the brethren who fear God and who are instructed by God directly. This kind of jurist attempts to contend against them in a field of knowledge of which he has no inkling of the first principles. Were any of them to be questioned about some term employed by the gnostics they would soon display their ingorance on the subject. If they would only reflect on God's saying, 'Here you are disputing on something of which you know nothing',[1] they would consider the matter more carefully and repent.

The Prophet himself censured those of the learned who sought knowledge for other than God's sake or who excercised it in ways displeasing to God. It is clear that he did not censure them simply because they were learned, since he praised those who seek knowledge in the fear of God.

In the same way I have censured certain Sufis; not the sincere ones, but only those who affect before men a holiness which is contradicted by their true condition. God says, 'There are those whose eloquence amazes men in this world's life, but God knows well what is in their hearts.'[2] I do not therefore take the whole of the legal profession to task, since the Prophet said, 'Whom God wishes well He causes him to have knowledge of the Faith.'[3] However, the jurists I have mentioned are dominated by their egotistical and lustful desires, being in the grip of Satan. Since they continually offend against the Friends of God, they shall surely perish by their own testimony, as will be shown later.

As for those of the learned who are truly and deeply rooted in religious knowledge, they are the rightly guided, the torches of guidance, the models of piety, heirs to the Messenger of God in knowledge, works, sincerity and character, who properly merit the name of righteous. When you therefore hear me censure the

[1] Qur'an, III, 65. [2] Qur'an, II, 204. [3] Bukhari, *'Ilm*, 10.

jurists, I mean only those who are led by their selfish and lustful desires. Likewise, in censuring certain of the Sufis, I mean the kind I have mentioned above, since the incarnationists[1] and free-thinkers[2] who attach themselves to our Way are in fact the fellow-travellers of Satan and abetters of perdition. May God illuminate our inner sight and theirs, may He restore our inner hearts and theirs and cause them to awaken to their errors so that they may return to the straight path.

In connection with the above-mentioned Abū al-Ḥasan and my foregoing remarks concerning certain legists, it is interesting to note that when al-Mawrūrī, al-Ḥabashī and I went to visit him, one who had witnessed the working of his (the Shaikh's) spiritual power, his reaction was as follows: When the Shaikh al-Mawrūrī knocked on his door he called out and asked who was there. When he was told 'Abdallāh al-Mawrūrī there was a silence after which his son came out to tell us, firstly that his father was busy, and then that he was not available. Thus he pretended not to know who the Shaikh was, so far had his hatred of the brethren gone and so tainted had he become by the jurists. May God protect us from one who would sever us from Him, His Folk and His Élite.

Whenever this Abū al-Ḥasan met me he would rebuke me for associating with the Folk, saying, 'How can a fellow like you associate with the likes of them?' I retorted that such as I was not worthy even to serve them, since they were the true leaders of men. The only reason he sought me out was that I might help him in his studies and not because I was on the Way and loved its Folk. Finally I left him for God to deal with and severed my association with him. Today he thinks as other jurists do, that sanctity is a vain fancy and that none is known to possess it.

Whenever I hear a jurist talking about the miraculous deeds of the Saints, I press him for details of these things and then demonstrate these things to him in someone. Then he says, 'Who would be foolish enough to think this fellow genuine? If he were so, you would not have staged this demonstration. The

[1] The notion that God takes upon Himself human form is inadmissible in Islam and those few sects which adopted such doctrines were rejected by the Sufis, as here. Cf. Ḥujwīrī, *Kashf al-maḥjūb*, p. 260.

[2] Together with the religious authorities of orthodox Islam, the Sufis rejected all attempts to undermine the authority of Qur'anic doctrine and Apostolic Tradition by intellectual individualism.

whole thing is a hoax.' It is clear that such a man would think no good of anyone. I have never ceased to maintain the rights of the brethren against these jurists and I have always sought to guard and protect them. This I was inspired to do, for whoever sets out to rebuke the Saints generally or specifically and whoever, not having associated with them, attacks one who does, that person demonstrates his ignorance and will never gain salvation.

A certain judge, one 'Abd al-Wahhāb al-Azdī,[1] a jurist from Alexandria, talked with me one day in the Sanctuary at Mecca. The Devil had instilled into him the belief that the times were completely lacking in all spiritual degrees (of attainment) and that all claims to this effect were fabrications and superstition.[2] I therefore asked him how many lands belonged to the Muslims, to which he replied that there were many. Then I asked him how many of these lands he himself had visited, to which he replied that he had been in six or seven of them. Then I asked him how many people, in his opinion, lived in these lands, to which he replied that they were very many. Then I further asked him which were in the majority, the ones he had himself seen or those he had not seen, to which he replied that the majority were, without doubt, those he had not seen. Then I laughed and said, 'How smitten and stupid is one who thinks he has seen many when he has only seen a few and judges the many by the few, elevating such a judgement to the status of an expert opinion. Surely any thinking believer would admit that there might be one he hasn't seen, even from the few he thinks he has seen, and that that one might be blessed with spiritual attainment. How then is it possible to doubt the ignorance of one who admits he has only seen a few countries and even fewer people, and yet holds such a belief. God causes such a one to perceive only the deficiencies of this world and none of its good, so that, judging what he has not seen by what little he has seen he is wretched in the sight of God. In this connection one should consider God's saying, "Were you to obey most people in the

[1] Cf. *Futūḥāt*, II, p. 69. He met him in 599/1202–3.

[2] As in other religious traditions the spiritual life is divided into various stages and degrees of attainment. At the summit of this attainment stands the true saint to whose perfection all other men nominally or actively aspire. Cf. 'Abd al-Karīm al-Jīlī, *De l'Homme Universel*, trans. T. Burckhardt, Derain, Paris, 1953.

world, they would lead you astray from God'',[1] and ''. . . except those who believe and do what is good, few are they.''[2] Here God points out that the former are in the majority and the latter in the minority.'

This judge then proceeded to amaze us further, for I heard him say something which demolished his own intellectual position. He said, 'Men are of two kinds, the intelligent and the unintelligent. The unintelligent man is not worth talking to by reason of his deficiency, and the intelligent man is far from infallible, so nothing is reliable.' Consider how, in his wretchedness, this man sees nothing but deficiencies and drawbacks, not looking for the good at all. Does he not imply, in making the division, that the unintelligent man, because of his own deficiency, seeks instruction from the learned man, hoping that God will thus furnish him with knowledge? In fact the intelligent man is, for the most part, accurate in his judgements and, by reason of his intelligence, is usually satisfied only with clear proofs. If, after exercising his intelligence on a matter, he is still mistaken, he is either to be forgiven or he returns to the right way.

As for this man's self-contradiction, consider the saying of the Prophet regarding the ruler, 'If he exercises his own judgement and is right he has two rewards; if he does so and makes a mistake he has one reward.'[3] Thus everyone who uses his own intelligent judgement is right in some respect, since, in both cases, he is to be rewarded and not reprimanded. Whatever results is the will of God. For this reason did I consider the jurist exceedingly ignorant. Praise be to God, Lord of the Worlds.

FROM 'AL-DURRAT AL-FĀKHIRAH'[4]

Unique in his time for his great reliance upon God and his veracity, he was a companion to Abū Madyan, Ibn Saidabūn,[5] 'Abd al-Razzāq al-Mughāwir,[6] al-Kamāl and Abū 'Abdallāh b. Hasān.[7]

He kept company with me for a time. When I left him he was still living in his country.

[1] Qur'an, VI, 17.
[2] Qur'an, XXXVIII, 24.
[3] Bukhārī, *I'tiṣām*, 21.
[4] Esad Ef. 1777, f. 94a.
[5] *Futūḥāt*, II, p. 641.
[6] See above, p. 101, n. 3.
[7] See below, p. 158.

He had a daughter under one year of age. So influenced was she by his spiritual state that when the brethren had attended for the Invocation and had formed a large circle, she would jump down from her mother's lap and stand in the middle of the circle on her legs. At such times ecstasy would overcome her. Even at so tender an age she manifested things which made it apparent that God had placed a light in her heart by which she had spiritual knowledge. She died before she was weaned.

One night I was with him in the house of Abū 'Abdallāh Muḥammad al-Khayyāṭ, whom I have already mentioned.[1] There was present with us a certain Muḥammad al-Baskarī, the purity of whose doctrines we suspected since he adhered to the doctrines of the ancients. There were also with us that night Aḥmad al-Lawshī, Muḥammad b. Abū al-Faḍl, Aḥmad al-Ḥarīrī b. al-'Assād[2] and Ibn al-Maḥabbah, all of them leaders in the Way. We were all sitting facing the *qiblah* and everyone had his head between his knees, practising Invocation or contemplation. Suddenly a sort of sleep overcame me and I saw myself and the whole company in a very dark room so that '. . . if a man were to stretch forth his hand he would scarcely be able to see it.'[3] From each of us there emanated a light from his essence to illuminate the darkness immediately around him. As we sat in the light of our own essence, a person came in to us through the door of that dark room and greeted us, saying, 'I am the apostle of the truth to you.' Then we asked him what he had to say of the man whose doctrines we suspected. He said, 'He is a believer in the Unity of God.' This was indeed true, but it was not this but his creed we suspected. Then I said, 'O Apostle, deliver the message you have been sent with.' He said, 'Know that good is in existence and evil in non-existence. God, in His generosity, has created man and has made him unique in His creation, created according to His Names and Attributes; but man has lost sight of this by regarding his own (individual) essence, seeing himself by himself and the number returns to its origin.[4] He is He and not you.' Then I returned to my senses from this vision and told the company what I had seen. They were pleased by it but not carried away. Then we all returned to our former state. I then applied myself to solving the meaning of what I had

[1] See above, p. 91. [2] See above, p. 95. [3] Qur'an ,XXIV, 40.
[4] The last word is illegible in the manuscript.

seen and composed some verses on the subject, all of which I did silently within myself. Then al-Mawrūrī came to himself and called to me, but I did not answer. Then he said, 'Answer me, for you are awake and are working out some verses on the Unity of God Most High.' At this I raised my head and said to him, 'How did you know this?' He answered, 'Your eye is open and you are making fast the hunters' net.' I said, 'The setting in order of strewn beats is the same as the setting in order of scattered words, which is poetry; its coming into being is the net of the hunter. Only that which has life (spirit) is caught in the net, and speech and poetry have no life except they are of God. As for his faith in the divine Unity, I knew it was innate in him, may God be pleased with him.'

One day we were on a journey with him when we came to some bitter salty water, unfit for use. He pronounced the Name of God Most High and then offered us some of the water to drink and we found it sweet and wholesome. I have also witnessed the contraction of the earth effected by this man's spiritual power (*barakah*). Once we saw a high mountain in the far distance, some days' journey away, become as near as a single step; so that by our taking a single step it lay behind us at the same distance. He was not present with us at the time.

---

15 ABU MUHAMMAD 'ABDALLAH AL-BAGHI AL-SHAKKAZ[1] of Priego

He came from the citadel at Priego to live in Granada where he has been till now (A.D. 1202–3).

One day I visited him with my companion al-Ḥabashī. Since it was my custom, whenever I visited a Shaikh or one of the brethren, to give him all the money I had on my person, I handed him the single dirham I had in my purse.

He was a most earnest man, usually to be found in a sad and tearful state. He hated sin as he hated unbelief and hated venial sins as much as greater ones. He had attained to the station of Preservation, being almost entirely free from sin of any kind:

[1] Cf. *Futūḥāt*, II, p. 187; IV, p. 9. They met in Granada in 595/1199.

as Ibn 'Uqqāl[1] said of his own Shaikh, 'I was always with my Shaikh Hārūn and I never saw him commit a major sin. However, my Shaikh would sometimes sleep the whole night through which caused me doubts regarding his spiritual effort. Then an inner voice said to me, "Do those who commit evil deeds imagine that we have made them like those who believe and do good, or that their lives and deaths are to be judged in the same way? How ill they consider. 'Then I came to my Shaikh and asked him if he had ever committed a major sin, to which he replied that he had not even committed a minor sin knowingly.'

This Shaikh of ours spent his nights in worship and his days in fasting. No postulant could keep company with him because he would demand of them the same standards of spiritual exertion he imposed on himself, which frightened them away. He lived completely alone and had no mercy on himself. When it was pointed out to him that the Companions of the Prophet were more lenient towards themselves, he replied, 'If they had nothing else to their credit than the holy company they kept, when could we ever hope to attain to their station?'

I know none to compare with this man, except perhaps Abū Muslim al-Khawlānī, one of the followers.[2] His earnestness and endeavour were such that he would cut and prepare sticks for the purpose of beating his legs whenever they grew weary of standing in prayer. At such times he would say to his legs, 'You are more worthy of a thrashing than my riding beast', continuing in this fashion until all the sticks were broken.[3] Then he would say, 'Do the Companions of the Prophet think that they can have Muḥammad all to themselves? By God, I will draw closer and closer to him till they realize that there are those who have come after them who are worthy of his company.'

He was a witty man and pleasant to associate with. He regretted much, and was very fond of spiritual allusions. He would say, 'Consider well the following four categories of men: ". . . those who are true to their contract with God",[4] ". . . whom neither commerce nor business diverts from the remembrance

[1] A Sufi of the Maghrib.
[2] Ibn 'Arabī's uncle. See above, p. 21.
[3] Cf. *Futūḥāt*, II, p. 18.
[4] Qur'an, XXXIII, 23.

of God",[1] ". . . those on the Heights"[2] and ". . . men will come to you on foot".'[3]

16 ABU MUHAMMAD 'ABDALLAH AL-QATTAN

This man had a profound understanding of the Qur'ān and was a blameless man who spoke the truth without fear. Even rulers were not immune from the severity of his denunciations and he would present the truth forcefully to all without exception. It did not in any way concern him that by denouncing the misdeeds and unlawful exploits of the Sultans he exposed himself to the danger of execution. He had many confrontations with rulers, but the exigencies of space prevent me from relating them. He used to quote only from the Qur'ān and ignored all other books. On one occasion in Cordova I heard him say, 'Poor wretches they who compile books and essays, for how great a reckoning they will have to face on the morrow. Are not the Book of God and the Traditions of His Messenger sufficient for them?'

He would always look after his companions, although he himself never lived in comfort and hardly had two dirhams to rub together.

One day a certain Sultan decided to have him executed; so the guards seized him and brought him before the Vizier (*wazīr*). The Shaikh then said to him, 'O oppressor, O enemy of God, O enemy of your own soul! Why am I being charged?' The Vizier replied, 'God has put you in my power and you will not live for more than a day.' Then the Shaikh said, 'It is not within your power to hasten or delay an appointed moment. Indeed none of what you threaten me with will come to pass, for it is I who will attend at your last rites.' Then the Vizier ordered his guards to throw the Shaikh into prison until he had consulted the Sultan concerning his execution.

As he was being taken off to the prison for the night, he said, 'The true believer is always in prison in this world, and this

[1] Qur'an, XXIV, 37. [2] Qur'an, VII, 46.

[3] Qur'an, XXII, 27. Cf. *Futūḥāt*, IV, p. 9. The four categories of men described in the Qur'anic quotations denote the apostle (*rasūl*), the prophet (*nabī*), the Saint (*walī*) and the believer (*mu'min*).

prison is merely part of the greater one.' On the next day, when the Vizier had told the Sultan about the Shaikh and his utterances, the Sultan ordered him to be brought before him. When he had been brought the Sultan saw before him an ugly man for whom nobody cared and whom no-one wished well, all because he spoke the truth and brought to light the faults and misdeeds of men. After he had asked of the Shaikh his name and lineage, the Sultan asked him whether he had preserved his belief in the Unity of God, whereupon the Shaikh recited some of the Qur'ān to him and expounded its meanings. The Sultan was impressed by this and warmed to him; so much so that he began to discuss matters of state with him. The Sultan asked the Shaikh what he thought of his dominion, at which question the Shaikh laughed out loud. On being asked the reason for his laughter the Shaikh said, 'You call this mad folly you are in a dominion and you call yourself a king. You are more like he of whom God said, "There was a king coming after them plundering all their ships",[1] which king now suffers punishment and burns in the fire. You are like the man for whom a loaf is kneaded and who is then told to eat it.' Then the Shaikh became scathing in his denunciation, unleashing his anger on all which angered him, there being ministers and jurists present. The Sultan then fell silent in shame and said, 'This is a man who speaks aptly. O 'Abdallah, become a member of our court.' At this the Shaikh said, 'Never; for your court and your palace are wrongfully acquired and, had I not been compelled, I would not have come here at all. May God preserve me from you and all like you.' Then the Sultan ordered him to be given gifts and pardoned. As for the Shaikh, he returned the gifts and accepted the pardon. The Sultan then ordered that the gifts be given to his family. Before much time had passed the Vizier died and al-Qaṭṭān attended his funeral, saying, 'My oath is fulfilled!'

He would often shout and raise his voice before the nobles of the land, saying, 'These are the wrong-doers who perpetrate injustice in the land. May the curse of God, of men and of angels be on them for ever and ever. Their punishment will not be lightened nor shall they be granted any respite.'

I myself used to associate with this man and he had great affection for me. On one occasion I invited him to spend the

[1] Qur'an, XVIII, 79.

night at our house. After he had been seated my father, may God have mercy on his soul, came in. My father was one of the Sultan's men,[1] but when he entered the Shaikh greeted him, since he was an old man. When we had performed the prayer I brought food for the Shaikh and sat down to eat, my father joining us in order to benefit from the Shaikh's spiritual grace. After a while the Shaikh looked at him and said, 'O unhappy old man, is it not time you felt some shame before God? How long are you going to associate with these oppressors? How shameless you are! How can you be sure that death will not come upon you in your evil state?' Then, pointing to me, he said, 'There is a lesson for you in your son, for here is a young man with all his bodily appetites in full bloom, who has nevertheless subdued his lusts, cast out his devil, turned to God and associates with God's people, while you, an old man, are on the brink of the abyss,' My father wept at his words and realized plainly his plight. As for myself, I was completely taken aback by all this.

These are merely some of the many tales I could tell of this Shaikh.

I introduced him in Cordova to my companion al-Ḥabashī and we walked with him to his house. I heard him say one day, 'I am amazed at one who wants a horse before he has begun to thank God for his food and clothing.' He himself never had more than the bare necessities by way of food or clothing. He was the scourge of tyrants and attended all raids into Christian territory, on foot and without provisions.

---

17 'ABDALLAH IBN JA'DUN AL-HINNAWI B. MUHAMMAD B. ZAKARIYA[2] the Henna Collector

He died in Fez in the year 597/1200–1. I brought him together with my companion al-Ḥabashī. This Shaikh was one of the

[1] His father was in government service. According to al-Qārī al-Baghdādī he was Vizier to Ibn Mardanīsh, the ruler of Murcia who was overthrown by the Almohads in 568/1172. Cf. *Manāqib Ibn 'Arabi*, ed. Munajjīd, p. 22.

[2] He is briefly mentioned in the *Futūḥāt*, II, p. 7.

four Supports (*awtād*) through whom God preserves the world.[1] He had asked God to remove his good repute from the hearts of the world. When he was absent he wasn't missed and when he was present no-one sought his advice; when he arrived in a place he was accorded no welcome and in conversation he was passed over and ignored.

I do not now remember the reason for my meeting with him. That is because, when I came to the city of Fez, certain people who had heard of me wished to see me. I therefore fled from the house where I was staying and took refuge in the Friday mosque. These people went to the house and when they did not find me there they came to the mosque. I saw them and they came to me and asked for Ibn 'Arabī so I told them to look further until they found him.

As I was sitting there, clad in worldly clothes, the Shaikh suddenly appeared before me. I had never seen him before that time. He greeted me and I returned the greeting. Then he opened al-Muḥāsibī's book *On the Exposition of Gnosis,* read a few words from it and asked me to give him an interpretation.[2] Through divine inspiration I had been told who he was, what was his spiritual station, that he was one of the four Supports and that his son would inherit his position. I therefore told him that I knew who he was and spoke his name. Thereupon he closed the book, stood up and said, 'Be most discreet about this, for I like you and would like to know you better. Your purpose is sound.' Then he left me. After that I sat in session with him only when no one else was present.

He suffered from a tied tongue and spoke only with great difficulty, but when he recited the Qur'ān his delivery was excellent. His spiritual work was great and he earned his living as a henna siever.[3] He always appeared dishevelled and

[1] This relates to the teaching that God maintains each cosmic sphere through the instrumentality of some appointed being whose function is usually of an entirely spiritual nature which is rarely, if ever, apparent to the senses. Each sphere as also each period has its own hierarchy of divine agents. At the head of each is the Pole (*quṭb*) who has under him Supports (*awtād*), Substitutes (*abdāl*) and others who aid him in his work of preservation. Abū Madyan was widely regarded as the Pole of his time. Cf. E. Blochet, 'Études sur l'ésoterisme musulman', *Journal Asiatique,* XIX, 1902, pp. 528 f., and XX, 1902, pp. 49 f.

[2] For al-Muḥāsibī, see above, p. 87, n. 5. A manuscript of the work mentioned here, *Sharḥ al-ma'rifah* is to be found at the British Museum, Or. 4026.

[3] Henna was used as a cosmetic dye.

dusty, his eyes annointed with antimony because of the henna dust.

FROM AL-DURRAT AL-FĀKHIRAH'[1]

. . . If he spoke he appeared foolish, when he sat down others began to get up and leave and when he was present in a company the others found his presence tiresome. This state of affairs was pleasing to him.[2]

One day I was sitting by the minaret when Ibn Ja'dūn came and sat down in front of me after greeting me. Then he opened al-Muḥāsibī's book, *The Exposition of Gnosis*, read from it and asked me to comment on what he read, which I did. Finally I said to him, 'Fellow, if you don't stop this I will reveal your position to the people, for you are one of the four (Supports).' At this he asked me to conceal his identity and promised to do the same for me.

---

18 ABU 'ABDALLAH MUHAMMAD B. ASHRAF AL-RUNDI[3] of Ronda

He was one of the seven Substitutes.[4] He kept to the mountains and coasts and avoided the inhabited areas for nearly thirty years. He was profound in his spiritual insight, given to weeping, prayer and fasting. Often, while engrossed in contemplation, he would write with his finger in the dust and then raise his head and breathe deeply which produced a droning noise in his chest. His ecstasy was intense and his tears copious.

I used to associate with him and keep company with him which used to cheer him and cause him happiness. He came from a rich and noble family.

[1] Esad Ef. 1777, f. 101b.

[2] Cf. above, p. 115, n. 1. Since this Shaikh's function as one of the Supports is of a hidden nature and does not involve external activity, the anonymity and lack of attention described both here and in the passage (above) from the *Rūḥ al-quds* constitute a providential protection for that function from outside interference.

[3] Cf. *Futūḥāt*, II, p. 7.

[4] See above, p. 115, n. 1.

One day I set out from Sidonia, making for the coast in search of other brethren. A certain beardless youth who sought association with me followed me, so I took him with me. On the way there appeared in front of us two men; one of them, tall and brown, was ‘Abd al-Salām the Wanderer who wandered from place to place,[1] and the other a man known as Muḥammad b. al-Ḥājj of the Banū Jawād. Although they were walking at a good pace and were a mile distant from us, I caught up with them and passed them by, walking very quickly. Since it was Friday, I stopped at the village of Rota to attend the Friday prayer.[2] I entered the mosque of the community and performed two cycles (*rak‘āt*) of the prayer.[3] This mosque was much frequented by the pious at night, since it was the hospice of Ḥasan, a man famed for his spiritual grace. In this place something very interesting happened.[4]

I had not been there very long before Ibn Ashraf arrived. As he entered the mosque the two men I had passed on the road recognized him and greeted him. While this was going on I was reclining in the mosque, beating my breast with my hand and singing some verses:

Displaying teeth like pearls,
Revealing the fullness of His face.
Time cannot hold Him,
But my breast encloseth Him.[5]

Then the Shaikh came over to me, drew me up and said, ‘Are you trying to conceal who you are?’ to which I replied, ‘Are you not trying to do the same?’ This was in fact the case.

The village headman came to me and invited me to break my fast with him and to bring anyone else I wished; but the Shaikh

[1] Such men were mendicants who were supported by the offerings of the pious. See below, p. 138.

[2] Friday is the day on which Muslims congregate in the mosque to perform the midday prayer and to hear a sermon (*khuṭbah*). It is not a sabbath in the ordinary sense, since the people return to their work after the prayer. Cf. *Encyclopaedia of Islam*, art. *Salat*.

[3] See above, p. 85, n. 1.

[4] This pilgrimage to Rota took place in 590/1193 after his return from Africa (see above, p. 28). On his way he had an encounter with al-Khiḍr, the spiritual patron of saints (see above, p. 29).

[5] A reference to a Tradition of the Prophet, ‘My heaven and My earth do not contain Me, but the heart of My faithful servant contains Me.’

said to me, 'Don't eat that sort of food; rather follow the brethren. When they eat, come and break your fast with me.' This I did.

He told me many things and promised that I would meet him again in Seville. After staying with him for three days I left that place. Before I took my leave of him he told me exactly what would happen to me after my departure, all of which subsequently took place.

After my arrival in Seville God put it into my head to go off and visit this Shaikh so that I might benefit further from his company. The day was a Tuesday and my mother had given me permission to go. The next morning there was a knock on the door and on answering it I found a man from the wilderness standing outside. He asked me whether I was Muḥammad b. al-'Arabī. When I told him that I was the person for whom he was looking he said, 'While I was walking somewhere between Marchena and Purchena I met a man of awesome appearance with a muttering voice who asked me whether I was bound for Seville. When I said that I was going there he asked me to call at the house of Muḥammad b. al-'Arabī and to tell him that his companion al-Rundī sends his greetings. I was also to tell him that at the same moment in which he receives the greetings it will occur to him to go to Tunis. Furthermore, I was to tell him to proceed thence in peace and that he would meet him, God willing, on his return to Seville.'

It was as he had said, for on the very next day I travelled to see you in Tunis and was away from Seville for a while.[1] One or two days after my return to Seville I met with al-Rundī and spent the night with him at the house of Abū 'Abdallāh al-Qasṭīlī.[2]

One of the things for which he was well known was his practice of sitting on a high mountain near Moron. One night a man was on the mountain and saw a shimmering pillar of light so bright he could not look at it. When he approached it he found that it was al-Rundī standing in prayer. The man went away and told people what he had seen.

He earned his living as a gatherer of camomile in the mountains which he sold in the city.

I myself witnessed many wonders performed by him. Some

[1] See above, p. 17. [2] See below, p. 138.

brigands once came upon him sitting by a spring and threatened him with death unless he stripped off his clothes. At this he wept and said, 'I cannot bring myself to assist you in disobeying God, so if you want this you must do it yourselves.' Then he was seized by an intense fervour and looked at them with his well known look and they fled from him.[1]

One day, while we were walking together by the sea, he asked me a question concerning God's saying, 'I require no provision from them, nor do I need them to feed Me.'[2] I did not answer him, but left him. Four years later I met him and told him that I had the answer to his question. He said, 'Let me have your answer, for after four years the time is ripe for it.' I then gave him my answer and marvelled that he had remembered the verse.[3]

It had long been my wish to introduce my companion al-Ḥabashī to him, so when we came to Andalusia we stayed at Ronda. While we were there we attended a funeral service, during the course of which I noticed that al-Rundī was standing in front of me. Then I introduced my companion to him and we all went back to the place where I was staying. Al-Ḥabashī expressed a wish to see some evidence of al-Rundī's miraculous powers. Later, when we had performed the sunset prayer, the owner of the house was late in lighting the lamp and my friend called for light. Al-Rundī said that he would oblige him. Thereupon he took a handful of grass which was lying about in the house and as we watched, struck it with his forefinger saying 'This is fire!' Immediately the grass burst into flames and we lit the lamp. He would sometimes take some fire from the stove with his hand for some purpose or other and, although some of it would stick to him, it caused him no pain or harm.

He was an illiterate man. One day I asked him about his

[1] Anger, when it expresses opposition to evil and when it transcends individual considerations is a virtue, 'anger in God'.

[2] Qur'an, CI, 57.

[3] This seemingly incomprehensible incident illustrates an important feature of spiritual development. By asking the question of Ibn 'Arabī the Shaikh causes him to become aware of the text, the inner truth of which requires time to mature in his soul. Thus, some four years later, Ibn 'Arabī is ready to answer the question properly, since the spiritual grace attaching to the text has done its work in him. Thus neither the timing of the question nor that of the answer were in any way fortuitous. The incident further illustrates the intimate and very special relationship between the master and the disciple.

weeping, to which he replied that he had sworn never again to invoke God's curse against any man; he had done so once and the man had perished, which he had deeply regretted ever since. He was a mercy to the world. More than this I cannot tell at the present time.

FROM 'AL-DURRAT AL-FĀKHIRAH'[1]

We were once praying with him outside Marchena when some dispute arose as to the direction of Mecca. He then pointed out the correct direction with his finger saying, 'There is the Ka'bah!' Then we prayed and I saw the sacred House and the people performing their circumambulations round it; indeed I even saw someone of my acquaintances among those close to the Ka'bah. We prayed then in certainty. When we had finished the prayer the Ka'bah vanished.[2]

He once have me three dirhams wrapped in a long lock of hair. I kept it very safely, for I was travelling by night with it in my pocket. As I was walking along the road I heard the sound of men. The place was a perilous one. When I went towards them I found a group of men, one of whom was afflicted with a violent pain. They begged me in the name of God to use some spell to cure him of the pain. I then remembered one of our leading Shaikhs' saying that if a genuine dirham were placed on the place of the pain, relief would soon follow. I therefore took out one of the dirhams and told his companions to place it on the spot where the pain was felt. As soon as they had done so the pain ceased and the man got up and walked off with his companions. Before they left they asked me to let them have the dirham. I agreed to this and set off again on my journey. When I arrived at my house in Seville, Muḥammad al-Khayyāṭ and his brother Aḥmad, whom I have already mentioned, came to see me.[3] They said to me, 'We saw that you had arrived last night, but we have nothing with which to provide you with

[1] Esad Ef. 1777, bf. 95b.

[2] The Ka'bah is the cube-shaped building in Mecca at the centre of the Sanctuary, towards which all Muslims turn when they pray. Cf. *Encyclopaedia of Islam*, art. *Ka'ba*. For an account of its symbolism in Sufi teachings, cf. F. Meier, 'The Mystery of the Ka'ba', *The Mysteries* (Papers from the Eranos Year Books), New York, 1955, pp. 149–68.

[3] See above, p. 91.

hospitality; so give us the two remaining dirhams to buy the evening meal with.' There are many other things I could relate about this Shaikh.

---

19 MUSA ABU 'IMRAN AL-SADRANI

This Shaikh came from Tlemcen and, although unknown, was one of the seven Substitutes and had many wonders to his name.[1]

My meeting with him came about as follows: One day, during the lifetime of Abū Madyan, after I had performed the sunset prayer in my house at Seville I had a great desire to see the Shaikh Abū Madyan who was at Bugia, some forty-five days journey away. After the sunset prayer I performed two cycles of the superrogatory prayer and, as I was saying the ritual greeting (*taslīm*), Abū 'Imrān came in and greeted me.[2] I sat him down next to me and enquired where he had come from, to which he replied that he had come from Abū Madyan at Bugia. Upon my asking him when he had been with him, he replied that he had only just finished praying the sunset prayer with him. He told me that Abū Madyan had said to him, 'Certain things have occurred to the mind of Muḥmmad b. al-'Arabī at Seville, so go at once and answer him on my behalf.' Then Abū 'Imrān mentioned the wish I had had to meet Abū Madyan and told me that Abū Madyan had said, 'Tell Ibn al-'Arabī that as for our meeting together in the spirit, well and good, but as for our meeting in the flesh in this world, God will not permit it. Let him however rest assured, for the time appointed for him and me lies in the security of God's mercy.' After that Abū 'Imrān talked to me on other matters and then returned to Abū Madyan.[3]

Shaikh Abū 'Imrān had formerly been a rich man, but had renounced his wealth. Eighteen days after his renunciation God inspired him with great spiritual knowledge. He became

[1] See above, p. 115, n. 1. Cf. *Futūḥāt*, II, p. 7. He met him in Seville in 586 H.

[2] See above, p. 85, n. 1.

[3] The visit described here must have been of a spiritual nature. In most religious traditions such phenomena were accepted as a feature of certain spiritual conditions.

one of the Substitutes and could locate himself in any place on earth he wished to be in.

Once he was denounced to the Sultan who ordered him to be seized. Accordingly he was taken, bound in iron chains and taken to Fez. When they were almost there, he was taken to a house and thrown into a room which was then locked and a guard put on the door for the night. In the morning they opened the door and found the chains on the floor, but no sign of Abū 'Imrān. He had meanwhile made his way to Fez where he sought out the house of Abū Madyan. When he found it he knocked on the door and Abū Madyan himself came to answer it. When Abū Madyan asked him who he was, Abū 'Imrān replied, 'I am Mūsā.' Abū Madyan then said, 'I am Shu'aib, so come in and fear not, for you are safe from the oppressors.'[1]

My Shaikh Abū Ya'qūb al-Kūmī[2] told me that Abū 'Imrān had once reached the mountain of Qāf which surrounds the earth and that he had performed the forenoon prayer at its base and the afternoon prayer at its summit.[3] On being asked the height of the mountain he had replied that it was three hundred years' journey high. He had also said that God had girded the mountain with an enormous serpent whose tail and head were joined. Abu 'Imrān's companion on this journey had said to him, 'Greet the serpent and it will return your greeting.' Abū 'Imrān had therefore greeted the serpent, whereupon the serpent had returned his greeting and enquired about Abū Madyan. Then he had asked the serpent how it came to know of Abū Madyan. The serpent replied, 'I am surprised at you! Is there anything on the earth which does not know of Abū Madyan? I and others have known him ever since God revealed His love and proclaimed it; indeed all things, animate and inanimate, know and love him.'[4]

In a certain country Abū 'Imrān had seen ants as large as goats and had met an old woman of Khurasān who stood on the

[1] An allusion to the Qur'an, XXVIII, 25.

[2] See above, p. 69.

[3] Jabal Qāf, like the Hindu Mt Meru and the Tibetan Mt Kailase, is regarded as the axis of the world. Cf. *Encyclopaedia ofIslam*, art. *Kāf*. The same story is told on p. 682 of the second volume of the *Futūḥāt*.

[4] Abū Madyan enjoyed a very high spiritual degree of attainment, being the Pole (*quṭb*) (see above, p. 115, n. 1) of the time. The saint who has come to know God in all things and all things in God is in harmony with all beings and is sought out as a channel of divine grace.

sea while the waves washed round her legs, praising and glorifying God.

This Shaikh's spiritual influence was very great and it would take far too long to tell all there is to tell concerning him.

---

20 ABU MUHAMMAD MAKHLUF AL-QABA'ILI

He lived in Cordova and died there after first seeking the permission of the Messenger of God, the peace and blessing of God be upon him. I once took my late father to see him so that he might pray for him. He kept us at his house from the morning until after the afternoon prayer and we had a meal with him.

As soon as one entered his house one felt the power of his spiritual presence before one actually saw him. When one did see him he was wonderful to look upon. He wore coarse wool, and, apart from various litanies and invocations, he would say a thousand times a day each, 'Glory be to God', 'God is the greatest', 'There is no god but God', and 'Praise be to God', being constantly engaged in Invocation.[1] His supplications embraced all things in heaven and earth, even the fishes of the sea. He was also much given to weeping.

Once he wanted to dig a well in his house and he was brought a foreign prisoner to help him with the operation. The Shaikh said, 'This man has been sent to help us, so we must pray to God that he embrace Islam.' Accordingly, when night came, the Shaikh secluded himself to pray for the man. When he came the next morning to do the work he announced that he had become a Muslim. When he was questioned about it he said that the Prophet had appeared to him in his sleep and had ordered him to believe in him and he had obeyed. Then the Prophet had told him that, because of the intercession on his behalf by Abū Muḥammad Makhlūf, he would accept him into Islam, or words to that effect.

[1] *Subḥān Allāh, Allāhu akbar, Lā ilāhā ill'Allāh* and *al-ḥamdu lillāh*, are frequently used in a similar way, not only by Sufis, but also by Muslims in general.

One day I left the company of the Shaikh and returned to my house, the Shaikh being in good health when I left him. That same night I dreamt that I was in open country with low-lying clouds overhead. Suddenly I heard the sound of neighing horses and the thundering of their hooves and saw a company of men, both mounted and on foot, descending from the skies in such numbers that they filled the heaven. I had never seen men with such fine faces, resplendent clothing and excellent horses. Then I saw in the midst of them a tall man with a large beard and silvery hair, his hand upon his cheek. I spoke to him and asked him the meaning of it all. He told me that the men I saw were all the prophets from Adam to Muḥammad. When I asked him who he was, he replied that he was Hūd of the people of 'Ad.[1] On my asking the purpose of their descent he told me that they had come to visit Abū Muḥammad in his sickness.

As soon as I awoke, I enquired about Abū Muḥammad and learned that he had fallen ill that very night. He lived a few more days and then died.

---

21 SALIH AL-KHARRAZ the Cobbler

A man from Seville who was most earnest in his worship of God. He had entered the service of God as a boy of only seven years. He used always to be engrossed in worship and never played games with the other boys or chattered with them. In his humility he worked as a cobbler to earn a living. He was devoted to his mother and, despite his tender years, copied out the whole of Ibn 'Assāl's great work.[2] He kept aloof from men and maintained long periods of silence. His companions said of him that he spoke to them only when it was really necessary.

I used to keep company with him and we had a great affection for each other. He would never retract what he had said, since he always spoke the truth. He would do nothing for those

[1] Cf. Qur'an, ch. XI, 'Hūd'.

[2] 'Abdallāh b. Faraḥ b. al-'Assāl lived at Toledo in the eleventh century A.D.

who knew him, lest they should think well of him. Most of the work he did was for strangers visiting the city, people who did not know him and whom he did not know.

One day one of our companions took to him a shoe which he had deliberately damaged in order to have the opportunity of talking to him. He greeted him and al-Kharrāz returned the greeting. Then our companion said to him, 'Would you please mend this shoe of mine?' al-Kharrāz said, 'I am busy with this shoe for which I have already been paid.' While all this was going on I was standing nearby where al-Kharrāz could not see me. Then our companion said to him, 'Keep it with you till you have finished the shoe you are mending,' to which al-Kharrāz replied, 'I might die before that time; don't you think you might take your shoe to someone else?' Our companion said, 'But I don't want anyone else to do the job for me', to which al-Kharrāz replied, 'You have heard what I said', and continued with his Invocation. Our companion then told him that he would sit there until he had finished, at which al-Kharrāz said, 'Do as you wish, but you have not heard my charge for the work yet.' Our companion then enquired what his charge might be and was told that it was an eighth of a dirham. He then offered al-Kharrāz a quarter, but was told that it was not a correct price. Then he told al-Kharrāz that it pleased him to pay that amount, only to have al-Kharrāz point out to him that he had earned sufficient for that day and that if he were feeling generous there were many people more needy than he. Despite further attempts, al-Kharrāz told him that he was being troublesome and that he would not do the work for him. He then continued with his devotions and his work.

The companion then came over to me in dismay. I told him that he had tried too hard and that he should go back and suggest to al-Kharrāz that he mend his shoe for God's sake and without charge. When he had done what I had told him, al-Kharrāz said, after a few moments silence, 'You have been sent by someone else with this suggestion.' Then he looked up and saw me. Finally he said to our companion, 'Leave your shoe with me and be off. Come for it later in the afternoon and if I am still alive I will return it to you; if I am dead I will leave it with a neighbour for you.' Then he looked at me and called me over to him. He said, 'Is this the way companions behave among themselves? Is it their practice to impose on their brothers what is not pleasing to them? Don't do this sort of thing again! But for the love which God has put in my heart for you, I would not have taken any notice of you, so preserve my anonymity, as I wish.'

I have never known one like this man. Later he went off into the wilderness seeking solitude and seclusion.

---

22 'ABDALLAH AL-KHAYYAT OR AL-QARRAQ

I met him at the Mosque of 'Udais in Seville when he was only ten or eleven years old. In appearance he was very shabby with a lean face, a thoughtful person, intense in his ecstasy and sadness.

Shortly before I met him I had received inspirations on the Way which nobody knew about. Therefore, when I saw him in the mosque I wanted to appear as his spiritual equal. I looked at him and he looked back at me and smiled. I then made a sign to him and he did the same to me. Then, suddenly, I felt like a fraud in his presence. He said to me, 'Be diligent, for blessed is he who knows for what he was created.' Then he performed the afternoon prayer with me, took his shoes, greeted me and was off. I went after him to find out where he lived, but I found no trace of him, nor could anyone tell me of his whereabouts. I have not seen or heard of him till this day. Some of the masters are young, some old.

---

23 ABU AL-'ABBAS AHMAD B. HAMMAM[1]

A man of Seville whom God inspired to discipline his soul. He began to devote himself to the worship of God before he reached puberty. He was a most earnest man who wept for

[1] He was also called al-Shaqqāq.

his soul like a mother who has lost her only son. His father had been opposed to his entering upon the Way, and when the situation became more difficult he said to me, 'O my brother, things have become very difficult for me; my father has thrown me out to fend for myself. I would very much like to go to the borders of the Muslim lands to fight the enemy and to serve there in the army until I die.' In due course he set off for a place called Jerumenha (in Portugal) and is still there to this day. After some time he returned to Seville to collect some effects, but then returned once again to active service. He used often to go to the house of the above-mentioned Abū 'Abdallāh al-Khayyāṭ, may God be pleased with them and us.[1]

---

24 ABU AHMAD AL-SALAWI
of Sale

He came to Seville while I was under the charge of al-Kūmī.[2] Abū Aḥmad's spiritual state was strong and he had spent eighteen years with Abū Madyan. His spiritual exertions were many, his devotion to worship firm and he was much given to weeping.

Once I kept company with him by night for a whole month in the Mosque of Ibn Jarrād. One night I got up to pray, performed the ritual ablutions and went up on to the roof of the mosque. There I found him sleeping at the roof door and I saw rays of light reaching from him to the sky. For a while I stood looking at him and I could not determine whether the rays came from him to the sky or from the sky to him. I stood there in wonder until he awoke from his sleep. He then performed the ablution and prayed.[3]

When he wept I would take the tears which had fallen on the floor and wipe them on my face, for I found that they gave off a scent like that of musk. People would smell it on me and say, 'Where did you buy such wonderful musk?'

[1] See above, p. 91.
[2] See above, p. 69.
[3] In the *Durrah* this story forms the account given of al-Salawī.

25 ABU ISHAQ B. AHMAD B. TARIF

He was the Shaikh of Abū 'Abdallāh al-Qurashī and came from Cairo. Gentle and mild in his manner, truthful and blameless in God's sight, given to zeal and spiritual endeavour, he would very much have liked to go into seclusion, but was prevented from doing so by his profession, which was the sale of earthenware. He copied many of the works written concerning the Way. He devoted himself to ascetic practices and spiritual learning.

His death came about in the following way: One day as he was walking in the street someone asked him, 'Was it so-and-so who passed you just now?' He was asking about a man of the locality whom God had afflicted with a disease of the throat which we called *al-naghnaghah*,[1] and whom the Shaikh did not know very well. When the man persisted in his questions, the Shaikh said, 'Do you mean the man with the diseased throat?' The man replied that it was. Sometime later the Shaikh said that at that very moment God called him inwardly and said, 'O Ibrāhīm, do you know our servants only by their afflictions? Has the man no name by which to call him? We will cause you to die by the very same disease.' By the next morning he had contracted the disease and died a short time afterwards.

His son Muḥammad told me this story at Mecca, telling me that his father had also said, 'I have not committed such a fault for twenty years.' I visited him twice and he liked me well. I met him in the company of al-Ḥabashī once at Ceuta and once in his own town.[2]

FROM 'AL-DURRAT AL-FĀKHIRAH'[3]

He lived at Jazīrat al-Khaḍrā[4] and was a companion to Abū al-Najāh, Abū al-Rabī', Ibn 'Abd al-Jalīl and Qaḍīb al-Bārr (al-Bān) who was at Mosul.[5]

One day he said to me, 'For me men are of two kinds: the friend who thinks well of me, who speaks what is good and who

[1] Goitre.
[2] See below, p. 129.
[3] Esad Ef. 1777, f. 99b.
[4] Near Algeciras.
[5] *Futūḥāt*, I, p. 187. Cf. below, p. 157.

deserves the name friend; and the one who speaks ill of me and makes known my spiritual state.'[1]

---

26 ABU MUHAMMAD 'ABDALLAH B. IBRAHIM AL-MALAQI AL-FAKHKHAR[2]
of Malaga

This man, who was known as the 'ship-caulker' (al-Qalafāt), was a companion of Abū al-Rabī' al-Kafīf and others and a friend of Ibrahīm b. Ṭarīf.[3] He followed the way of Chivalry (*futuwwah*) and showed all the signs of doing so.[4] One always saw him busy on someone else's behalf, he having no thought for himself. He would go to the authorities and rulers on behalf of others and his house was open to the poor. He adhered strictly to the law and behaved himself in a seemly way. Spiritually speaking, he was more joyous than Ibrāhīm b. Ṭarīf who was rather more stern in this respect. I met with this Shaikh on many occasions and he was very fond of me.

It happened one day at Ceuta, when he and Ibn Ṭarīf were there, that the Sultan Abū al-'Alī,[5] may God grant him success, sent two lots of food for us. I was not myself present at the time but the brethren who had come to that place to see me ate it, while my special companions did not partake of it. On the second night the Sultan did the same, but I myself neither accepted nor refused it. When they heard that the Sultan had sent down food, the brethren came to us to eat of it.

I, for my part, performed the night prayer. One of those who had come and who claimed to be a Shaikh, said to me,

[1] Among Sufis a respectful reticence is encouraged with regard to one's own spiritual condition or that of others, since it is a matter between God and His servant alone.

[2] Cf. *Futūḥāt*, I, p. 577.

[3] See previous piece.

[4] Chivalry for the Sufi meant the putting of others before oneself in all things, implying great forbearance and self-denial. Outside the Sufi ranks the term was applied to the qualities of hospitality, dignity and courage inculcated by a variety of craft and trading organizations similar to the early guilds. The members of these guilds were called *fityān*. Cf. *Encyclopaedia of Islam*, art. *Futuwwa*.

[5] This must be the Almohad Abū Ya'qūb.

'One may not pray on a full stomach.' I remained silent and did not answer him which made him angry; so I said to him, 'I did not accept the food, nor did I see fit to eat it because it is, in my opinion, unlawful food;[1] nor could I order you to eat it since I wish for you what I wish for myself.' Then, having explained to him the reason for my opinion regarding the food, I said, 'The food is available, so let him who considers it lawful eat it, otherwise not.'

Then I went into the house taking my special companions with me. In the morning that man went to the Vizier and told him that I had called them law-breaking people and other things. At this the Vizier was very angry and said, 'This is the man (meaning me) who accepted the sending of the food.' Then the charge was properly heard and finally reached the Sultan himself who was an intelligent man. The Sultan said, 'We only intended well by the food, but the fellow knows his own condition best, so we will do him no harm', whereupon he rejected the complaint.

Our companion al-Qalafāṭ[2] heard about the affair and came to see us. He feared for us all because of what he knew of the country and its ways. He said, 'This sort of behaviour is all right for yourself, but the harm resulting from it will rebound upon our whole company, for the people here do not lightly tolerate this sort of conduct. It is a saying in these parts, "Lowly is he who has no tyrant to help him, and in error is he who has no scholar to direct him aright." ' When I perceived that concern for mere men had swayed him and that he was anxious to effect a compromise for purely worldly considerations, I said, 'Wretched is he who relies upon the enemy of God. May God cease to care for the world if it ceases to show regard for His right, and it is His right which comes first.' Then I rose to my feet shaking my fist and he went away.

Sometime after this I met Ibn Ṭarīf. He had heard of the matter and said to me, 'Expediency would have been a better course', to which I replied, 'Yes, so long as the capital is preserved intact.' At this he fell silent.

[1] Ibn 'Arabī considered the food unlawful because it had been sent by a ruler. Cf. the above sketch on al-Qaṭṭān (p. 000) for an indication as to the attitude of the Sufis towards rulers and princes. The incident is alluded to in *Futūḥāt*, IV, p. 540.

[2] Namely, al-Fakhkhār.

Were it not for the dictates of space, I would have mentioned all our masters, but I have restricted it to these in order to keep this section short. I have devoted a whole book to them which I have called, *al-Durrat al-fākhirah,* this being a record of those from whom I have gained benefit on the path of the Hereafter.[1]

FROM 'AL-DURRAT AL-FĀKHIRAH'[2]

He came from Tarifa in Spain. He once told me that he had been in Mecca at the Ka'bah and met a certain non-Arab there. This man had seized him by the hand and enquired where he had come from. The Shaikh had told him that he was from a peninsula on the Atlantic Ocean. He then asked him if he knew what had brought them together in that place, at which the Shaikh asked him to say what it was. The man then replied, 'Heedlessness, my brother!' and then he wept.[3]

When I went to visit him I crossed the sea by night from Qaṣr Maṣmūdah[4] in the direction of Tarīfa. When morning came we were at a place called al-Safīḥah (al-Sanīḥah?). Then we sailed along the coast until we came to our destination. There we found this Shaikh standing on the shore with his followers asking about one who was coming to see him. He was told that he had just arrived in the boat. I got out of the boat and greeted him. He took me to his house and gave me the very food I had wished for while on the boat. When I asked him why he had prepared that food rather than any other, he told me that he had been informed inwardly that I was coming by sea to visit him and that I had a particular liking for that food, and that, accordingly, he had had it prepared for my coming. There are many things I could tell of this Shaikh.

[1] See Introduction.

[2] Esad Ef. 1777, f. 100a.

[3] For the Sufi the only true and worthwhile activity and preoccupation is *dhikr* or the Invocation of God's Name. The opposite of this is everything which deflects from that or deflects one from the awareness of God's all-embracing Unity. The implication of the remark quoted would seem to be that, ultimately, even sacred rites constitute a barrier to true awareness of God.

[4] Cf. *Levi-Provencal, La Peninsule Iberique au Moyen-age,* Leiden, 1938, p. 131.

27 'ABDALLAH B. TAKHMIST[1]

He was from Seville and was considered to be one of the Substitutes.[2]

FROM 'AL-DURRAT AL-FĀKHIRAH'[3]

He lived at Fez and was a companion to Abū Ya'izz.[4] He was generally thought to be one of the Substitutes. By profession he was a jurist and many closed doors of knowledge were opened to him. His presence always inspired awe and respect. Whenever we sat with him he would show his pleasure with me and smile at me.

One night he stayed so long in the Qarawiyīn mosque that the keepers closed the doors for the night. Therefore, when he had completed his superrogatory prayers and wanted to leave the mosque, he found all the doors locked. Then he murmured something softly and the door opened for him and he went off to his house.

28 A MAN CALLED AL-SAKHKHAN

He was one of the Substitutes who had fallen from grace so that he was in great grief and spoke to none. When I met him I was kind to him, because of his great distress.

29 ABU YAHYA B. ABU BAKR AL-SINHAJI[5]

The Shaikh, the gnostic, the wanderer, the recluse, the veracious, the righteous, a man versed in the spiritual mysteries—it

[1] The rest of the sketches are very brief. See above, p. 131, and the Introduction.
[2] See above, p. 115, n. 1.
[3] Esad Ef. 1777, f. 101a.
[4] This may be the same as Yūsuf b. Ta'izza, p. 134.
[5] Ibn 'Arabi has entered this Shaikh in the margin. He would seem to be the same as no. 134, above.

is very seldom one encounters such as he. He and I were concerned together with too many spiritual matters to mention here. It was for him that I composed *The Fabled Phoenix* concerning knowledge of the Seal of Saints and the Sun of the West.[1]

---

30 ABU AL-'ABBAS B. TAJAH

A man whose spiritual effort was considerable. The Qur'an was never absent from his hands until he died.

FROM 'AL-DURRAT AL-FĀKHIRAH'[2]

He was unable to restrain his tears whenever he heard the Qur'an recited. Whenever I sat in session with him he would ask me to recite the Qur'an to him. As a result of his extremes of devotion his body had become weakened and changed and his eyes ulcerous from his frequent weeping. He never missed the congregational prayer.

The time he allotted to me to sit with him was between noon and late afternoon in the Mosque al-Ḥamral (Jamral?) in Seville. During that time I would recite to him from the Qur'an, since his own sight had grown too weak to read the text himself. Many times God would give expression to my thoughts through his mouth.

When he was called by name he would neither raise his head nor take any notice of the person until he had greeted him properly and stated his purpose. Whatever advice he gave was couched in the words of the Qur'an. He always urged the contemplation of the Qur'an and the drawing of all knowledge from it, saying, 'Knowledge is a light which may only be had from the light which is the Qur'an *par excellence*. Just as a lamp is lit from another lamp, so does all knowledge derive

[1] This is his *'Anqa' mughrib* in which he discusses the question of the Seal of Saints (*khatm al-awliyā'*), both in its universal and strictly Muslim sense. Christ is given the title of the Seal of Saints in the universal sense. In the *Futūḥāt* he claims the title of the Seal of Saints for the Muslim tradition for himself. Cf. A. A. Afi, *The Mystical Philosophy of Muhiddin Ibnul Arabi*, Cambridge, 1939, p. 981.

[2] Esad Ef. 1777, f. 80a.

from the Qur'an, a light from light upon light.[1] My boy, God, may He be glorified, has taught us that He is the Light of the heavens and the earth, so that we might take our lights from Him; therefore seek light only from its true source.'

---

31 ABU 'ABDALLAH B. BISTAM AL-BAGHI of Priego

He came from Priego and was one who devoted himself to the reading of the Qur'an and to worship by night.

---

32 YUSUF B. TA'IZZA

He came from Carmona. He was so devoted to the reading of the Qur'an that he spoke to no man—an upright man who fasted much.

---

33 ABU AL-HASAN AL-QANUNI

He came from Ronda and was a follower of the way of Chivalry.[2] He was one versed in the sevenfold sciences.[3]

---

34 'O GOD, BLESS MUHAMMAD' AL-HADDAD

He was from Seville. He was famous for his tireless invocation of God's blessing upon the Prophet.[4]

[1] Cf. Qur'an, XXIV, 35. [2] See above, p. 129, n. 4.

[3] The seven sciences would seem to be the seven branches of gnosis enumerated by Ibn 'Arabī in his *Futūḥāt* (II, 393–422): (i) the divine Names; (ii) the divine Self-manifestation; (iii) revelation; (iv) perfection and imperfection in existence; (v) the essential man; (vi) the imagination (*Khayāl*); (vii) spiritual healing.

[4] The invocation of the blessing (*ṣalāh*) and peace (*salām*) of God upon the Prophet forms an integral part of Muslim worship. This is particularly the case in Sufism, since the Prophet is the spiritual prototype and bearer of the divine Word. Cf. F. Schuon, *Understanding Islam*, pp. 95–102.

35 ABU ISHAQ AL-QURTUBI of Cordova

One of the 'Believers'[1] and a companion of Abū Madyan of Bugia.

36 ABU 'ABDALLAH AL-MAHDAWI of al-Mahdiyah

He was from Fez. For a period of sixty years until he died he never turned his back on the *qiblah*.[2]

FROM 'AL-DURRAT AL-FĀKHIRAH'[3]

He lived in Fez for sixty-four years. He was very occupied with the salvation of his soul and I was told that he often suffered great anguish on this account.

I stood next to him in the mosque one day and he did not know me. I therefore pressed upon him in the row in which we were praying, so that I was partly sitting on him, and I behaved as badly as I could in such a place. Then he looked up at me and said, 'Behave yourself. You have plenty of room, so do not press upon me. I do not wish to fight with the likes of you.' Afterwards he warmed to me and I became his companion and benefited from his grace.[4]

37 'ALI B. MUSA B. AL-NAQARAT[5]

Although unknown by the brethren he was secretly a member of the order, his gnosis being complete and his insight (*firāsah*)[6]

[1] I do not know what is meant by the special use of the term 'believer' (*mu'min*) here.

[2] The *qiblah* is the direction of the Ka'bah at Mecca.

[3] Esad Ef. 1777, f. 101a.

[4] Cf. *Futūḥāt*, II, p. 15. He is not to be confused with Muhammad 'Abd al-'Aziz al-Mahdawī to whom the *Rūḥ al-quds* was addressed.

[5] Cf. Ibn Abbar, *Takmilah*, no. 1877. He was born in 515/1121 and died in 593/1197.

[6] Cf. *Encyclopaedia of Islam*, art. *Firāsa*.

considerable. He had little to do with others of the order till he died. He was well known for his recitations of the Qur'an and his readings of poetry.

38 ABU AL-HUSAIN YAHYA B. AL-SAIGH

He came from Ceuta, a Traditionist and a Sufi, which is a truly amazing combination.[1] He was a man as rare as pure gold and endowed with many spiritual graces. I associated with him often, communicating his works and studying with him.[2]

39 IBN AL-'AS ABU 'ABDALLAH AL-BAJI
of Beja

He lived in Seville and was both a jurist and an ascetic, which is an unusual combination.

40 ABU 'ABDALLAH B. ZAIN AL-YABARI
of Evora

He was from Seville, a man of great merit, much given to the practice of austerities. He studied the Qur'an and grammar at the Mosque of 'Udais in Seville. He was almost unknown and little noticed. He devoted himself to the study of the works of al-Ghazālī.[3]

[1] From the author's digression on the subject of jurists and scholars on p. 105, the reader will have understood that such people were not usually sympathetic towards those who followed the Sufi Way. A Traditionist is one who studies the Traditions of the Prophet.

[2] Cf. *Futūḥāt*, IV, p. 489.

[3] Al-Ghazālī was perhaps the greatest theologian of Islam, in addition to which he managed to bring Sufism and exoteric Islam closer together. His greatest work is the *Iḥyā' 'ulūm ad-dīn*, Cairo, 1939. He died in AD 1111. Cf. W. Montgomery Watt, *Muslim Intellectual*, Edinburgh, 1966.

One night he was reading the book of Abū al-Qāsim b. al-Ḥamdīn which attacks al-Ghazālī, when he was suddenly struck blind.[1] He immediately prostrated and abased himself, swearing that he would never again read the book. When he had put it away from him God restored his sight to him. He was one of the most meritorious of men. I also met his brother who was like him. When he died a cry was heard saying, 'Two of Paradise for the Sons of Zain!'[2]

FROM 'AL-DURRAT AL-FĀKHIRAH'[3]

He came from Evora, a town which is today in the hands of the Franks.

The same Ibn Ḥamdīn, who was the judge at Cordova, had al-Ghazālī's books burned and uttered anathemas against him. Sometime later Ibn Ḥamdīn saw al-Ghazālī in a dream with an iron chain in his hand with which he was pulling along a pig. Ibn Ḥamdīn relates that he greeted al-Ghazālī and enquired about the pig. Al-Ghazālī replied that the pig was Ibn Ḥamdīn and that he would remain in his power until he was shown how he had merited his curses.

41 ABU 'ABDALLAH AL-QAZZAZ

He was the Imām of the diseased at Cordova. He was a rare kind of man. On my asking him how he found life with these people, he replied that the only odour he could smell from them was the perfume of musk. I remember many wonders on his part.

42 ABU ZAKARIYA' YAHYA B. HASAN AL-HASANI

A man of Bugia, he was a leading scholar in government service, an ascetic and reverential man of good counsel. With his

[1] Ibn Ḥamdīn was a judge at Cordova. He died in AD 1127.
[2] The Arabic reads, *Jannatain ithnatain li-bani Zain.*
[3] Esad Ef. 1777, f. 107a.

permission I went into spiritual retreat with him and we questioned each other on spiritual matters.

He seemed to be dominated by the fear of God, being renowned for his austerities and the way he ate. I met with him on numerous occasions and studied some of his own compositions with him.

---

43 'ABD AL-SALAM AL-ASWAD the Negro

This man was an itinerant. Almost always when I came to a village, I would be told, 'So-and-so has passed through here.' He never settled in any place. When I asked him about his unsettled life he told me that he found a good spiritual state in moving about.

---

44 ABU 'ABDALLAH AL-QASTILI of Cazalla

He lived in Seville. He was an earnest and spiritually active man, most zealous for the Faith. Whenever I visited him I found him eager for prayer.

---

45 ABU AL-'ABBAS AHMAD B. MUNDHIR

He studied the Qur'an, language and Law, being alone in following the Mālikī school.[1] Among the wonders attributed to him was that, when a knotty problem presented itself to him, he would see Mālik himself solving it for him. Both spirits and men would resort to his house and pay their respects to him. Although he was rather poor, he once refused and returned some money which had been thrown to him.

[1] Anas b. Mālik was the founder of one of the four Sunnī Law schools. Cf. above, p. 83, n. 4.

46 MUSA THE TEACHER

He was a teacher in Fez. He was from the citadel of the Banū Sa'īd[1] and was one of the notables of Granada. His son 'Abdallāh grew up a pious boy, not knowing what sin was, a repentant youth who had never behaved as an ordinary child, being devoted to the study of the Book of God.

47 ABU AL-'ABBAS AL-KHARRAZ the Cobbler

I met him at Mecca. He had been a companion of 'Abdallāh al-Mughāwirī and passed on his teachings.[2] I derived much good from his supplications and saw many evidences of his spiritual grace.

48 AL-HAJJ ABU MUHAMMAD 'ABDALLAH AL-BURJANI of Purchena

This man, one of your friends and companions, is a man devoted to the emulation of the practice of the Prophet, a pious man of great worth and profound tranquility.

One day he asked me, regarding the verse, 'To whom We have brought the Book, which they recite as it should be recited,'[3] 'Why do they recite it properly?' I answered, 'O Abū Muḥammad, you tell me; you put the question and you should answer it.' Then he smiled and said, 'It is because it came when they had already been favoured with God's grace; thus, when they were given it they were assisted in reciting it.' This is indeed a rare allusion beneath which surge seas of knowledge for one who considers and reflects.[4] The Prophet said, concern-

[1] Alcala la real in the province of Jaen.

[2] Al-Mughāwirī was a noted Saint of Niebla near Seville.

[3] Qur'an, II, 121.

[4] Response to divine revelation is in accordance with a person's spiritual predisposition (*isti'dād*). Cf. Titus Burckhardt, *An Introduction to Sufi Doctrine*, Lahore, 1959, p. 134.

ing the office of Imām, 'If you are given it you will be assisted in it, but if you demand it you will not be assisted.'[1]

49 ABU 'ABDALLAH MUHAMMAD AL-NABILI

He lives in a cemetry. He is your servant whom God brought to the Way through you. The influence of your spiritual grace upon him is obvious. I witnessed many wonders on his part which I will not relate here, since there is no time to do so.

50 ABU 'ABDALLAH THE ALMORAVID

A man devoted to the Qur'an and to worship by night, in whom the lights of your grace are manifest, one sharp of mind and quick of understanding.

51 MAIMUN B. AL-TUNISI ABU WAKIL

He used to gather kermes for a living. While he was with us in Seville he fell ill. A certain pious lady, Zainab the wife of Ibn 'Aṭā' Allāh, took him into her house and nursed him. However, he died the night after he had been moved there. He was truly a man of God.

52 ABU MUHAMMAD 'ABDALLAH B. KHAMIS AL-KINANI[2]

He was a surgeon in Tunis. When I went to visit him in his house (*maḥras*) I made the journey bare-footed despite the intense heat, following the example of my two Shaikhs Abū

[1] I have not been able to trace this Tradition.
[2] Cf. *Futūḥāt,* I, p. 186.

Ya'qūb and Abū Muḥammad al-Mawrūrī[1] who told me that they had made their visit to him in this fashion. He was possessed of much spiritual grace, but you know of him well enough.

FROM 'AL-DURRAT AL-FĀKHIRAH'[2]

From Marsā Idūn in the region of Tunis. He was a prominent man among the people. He was one of the Shaikhs of 'Abd al-'Azīz al-Mahdawī[3] who, nevertheless, did not realize his true worth, since the Shaikh concealed much of himself from him. He was brought to the Way while attending the sessions of Abū Madyan. His spiritual attainments were such that Abū Madyan once said, when he was at Pechina, 'Had I wings (*janāh*) I would fly to al-Jarrāḥ.'

(There follows a more detailed account of his visit to this Shaikh bare-footed.) . . . When we had travelled half the distance, we met a man coming in the opposite direction who said to me, 'In the name of God, the Shaikh told me to meet you and tell you to put on your sandals again, because he knows of your intention (to visit him) and has prepared food for you.' When I arrived he came out to receive me at some distance from his house. He was leaning on a stick because of his advanced age. He showed great pleasure at seeing me. I sat with him for many days discussing the gnostic sciences. While I was there I saw a man walk on the sea without getting his legs wet, because of the grace of the Shaikh. I stayed in his company less than a year. Before I left he urged me not to tell 'Abd al-'Azīz al-Mahdawī of his true state, nor anyone else. He bade me also put it from my mind.

---

53 THE SEVEN PERSONS

I met them at Mecca, may God benefit all Muslims by them. I sat with them at a spot between the wall of the Hanbalites

[1] See above, p.39 , and p. 101.
[2] Esad Ef. 1777, f. 102b, where he is called Abū Muḥammad Jarrāḥ al-Murābiṭ.
[3] See above, p. 17.

and the bench of Zamzam.[1] They were indeed the elect of God. So overwhelmed were they by holy Tranquillity (*sakīnah*) and awe that they did not even blink their eyes. When I met them they were in a state of contemplation. No word passed between me and them on any matter, but I saw in them an almost unimaginable calm.

54 SHAMS, MOTHER OF THE POOR[2]

She lived at Marchena of the Olives where I visited her often. Among people of our kind I have never met one like her with respect to the control she had over her soul. In her spiritual activities and communications she was among the greatest. She had a strong and pure heart, a noble spiritual power and a fine discrimination. She usually concealed her spiritual state, although she would often reveal something of it to me in secret because she knew of my own attainment, which gladdened me. She was endowed with many graces. I had considerable experience of her intuition and found her to be a master in this sphere. Her spiritual state was characterized chiefly by her fear of God and His good pleasure in her, the combination of the two at the same time in one person being extremely rare among us.

FROM THE AL-DURRAT AL-FĀKHIRAH[3]

I first met her when she was in her eighties.

One day al-Mawrūrī[4] and I were with her. Suddenly she looked towards another part of the room and called out at the top of her voice, 'Alī, return and get the kerchief.' When we asked to whom she was speaking, she explained that 'Alī was on his way to visit her and that on his way he had sat down to eat by a stretch of water. When he got up to resume his journey he had forgotten the kerchief. This is why she had called out to him; he had gone back and had retrieved the kerchief. 'Alī was at that time well over a league away. After an hour he arrived

[1] This is a place close to the Ka'bah in the Sanctuary at Mecca. Cf. *Encyclopaedia of Islam*, art. *Mekka*.

[2] Her name was Yasmīnah. See above, p. 25. Cf. *Futūḥāt*, II, p. 35.

[3] Esad Ef. 1777, f. 986.

[4] See above, p. 103.

and we asked him what had happened to him on the way. He told us that he had stopped at some water on the way to eat and that he had then got up and left the kerchief behind. He went on to tell us that he had then heard our lady Shams calling him to return and get it, which he had done. She also had the power to voice the thoughts of others. Her revelations were true and I saw her perform many wonders.

55 NUNAH FATIMAH BINT IBN AL-MUTHANNA[1]

She lived at Seville. When I met her she was in her nineties and only ate the scraps left by people at their doors. Although she was so old and ate so little, I was almost ashamed to look at her face when I sat with her, it was so rosy and soft. Her own special chapter of the Qur'an was 'The Opening'. She once said to me, 'I was given "The Opening" and I can wield its power in any matter I wish.'[2]

I, together with two of my companions, built a hut of reeds for her to live in. She used to say, 'Of those who come to see me, I admire none more than Ibn Al-'Arabī.' On being asked the reason for this she replied, 'The rest of you come to me with part of yourselves, leaving the other part of you occupied with your other concerns, while Ibn al-'Arabī is a consolation to me, for he comes to me with all of himself. When he rises up it is with all of himself and when he sits it is with his whole self, leaving nothing of himself elsewhere. That is how it should be on the Way.'

Although God offered to her His Kingdom, she refused, saying, 'You are all, all else is inauspicious for me.'[3] Her devotion to God was profound. Looking at her in a purely superficial way one might have thought she was a simpleton, to which she

[1] Cf. *Futūḥāt,* II, p. 348.

[2] The actual words and sounds of the Qur'an are considered to have power of their own deriving from their divine origin. This accounts for the frequent use of texts from the Qur'an as charms and talismans. This view of the power of sacred texts and sounds corresponds to Hindu teachings on *Mantra.* Qur'an, I.

[3] An allusion to the teaching of the Sufis that even the worlds of the soul and spirit are ultimately illusory.

would have replied that he who knows not his Lord is the real simpleton. She was indeed a mercy to the world.

Once, on the night of the Festival, Abū 'Āmir, the muezzin, struck her with his whip in the mosque. She gave him a look and left the place feeling very angry with him. In the morning she heard him calling to prayer and said, 'O my Lord, do not rebuke me that I was affected by one who calls Your Name in the darkness of the night while other men sleep, for it is my Beloved who is mentioned on his lips. O God, do not censure him because of my feeling against him.'

The next morning the jurists of the locality went, after the Festival prayer, to convey their respects to the Sultan. This muezzin, full of worldly aspiration, went in with them. When the Sultan enquired who the fellow might be, he was told that it was only the muezzin. Then the Sultan asked who had allowed him to come in with the jurists and ordered him to be thrown out, which he was. However, after someone had pleaded with the Sultan for him he was let off, although the Sultan had intended to punish him. Fāṭimah heard about this incident and said, 'I know about it, and if I had not prayed for leniency for him he would have been executed.' Her spiritual influence was very great indeed. After this she died.[1]

FROM THE 'AL-DURRAT AL-FĀKHIRAH'[2]

Some of the believing *Jinn* would sit with her, seeking her companionship, but she would refuse them and ask them to remain hidden and would remind them of what the Apostle of God had said the night he caught the demon, 'I remembered the words of my brother Solomon and used them on it.'[3]

At first she had earned her living on a spindle. Then it occurred to her to earn her keep by hand-spinning, but God caused her spinning finger to become crippled from the moment she started on the work. I had noticed the finger and had asked her about it. She then told me the story and told me that she had, from that day relied upon the scraps of food thrown from

[1] At this point the biographical portion of the *Rūḥ al-quds* finishes.

[2] Esad Ef. 1777, f. 87a.

[3] In general, association of any kind with beings of a subtle nature is avoided by those with a genuine spiritual aspiration because of the dangers attaching to this realm. Cf. E. Underhill, *Mysticism*, VII.

people's houses. She came to the Way while still a young girl living in her father's house. I met her when she was already ninety-six years of age.

She had married a righteous man whom God had afflicted with leprosy. She served him happily for twenty-four years until he was taken to God's mercy. When she became hungry and no scraps or offerings of food came her way she would be content and thank God for His favour in that he was subjecting her to that to which He had subjected his prophets and Saints. She would say, 'O Lord, how can I deserve this great position in that You treat me as You treated Your loved ones?'

One day I built a hut for her of palm branches in which to perform her devotions. That same night the oil in her lamp ran out, something which had never happened to her before. I never learned the secret of that from her. She got up to open the door to ask me to bring her some more oil and, in the darkness, plunged her hand into some water in the bucket(?) underneath her.[1] At this she cursed and the water was immediately changed into oil. She then took the jug and filled it with the oil, lit the lamp and came back to see from where the oil had come. When she saw no further trace of oil she realized that it had been a provision from God.

One day when I was with her a woman came to see her to complain of her husband who had gone away to Sidonia, two days' journey from Seville.[2] She told us that her husband wanted to seek another wife in that place, which she found hard to accept. I asked Fāṭimah whether she had heard the woman's plea and begged her to call upon God to restore her husband to her. She said, 'I will make no supplication, but I will cause the chapter "The Opening" (*al-fātiḥah*) to follow behind him and bring him back.' I then said, 'In the name of God, the Merciful, the Compassionate', and she recited the rest of the chapter. Then she said, 'O chapter of "The Opening", go to Jerez de Sidonia to the husband of this woman and drive him back at once from wherever you find him and do not let him delay.' She said this sometime between noon and the late afternoon.

On the third day the man arrived at his home. Then the

[1] The word which I have translated as 'bucket' is illegible in the manuscript. My translation seems to fit what can be read.

[2] In the region of Jerez (Sharīsh).

woman came to inform us of his arrival and to thank us. I then told her to bring her husband to us. When he came we asked him what had brought him back from Jerez, when he had intended to marry and settle down there. He replied that he had left his house in the middle of the afternoon heading towards the municipal building for the marriage and that on the way he had felt a constriction in his heart and everything seemed suddenly very dark to him. At this he became very anxious. Then he left that place and arrived in Triana before sunset, where he had found a boat for Seville. Thus he had sailed the day before and had arrived in Seville that morning, having left all his baggage and effects behind in Jerez.[1] He admitted that he still did not know why he had done it. I have seen various miracles performed by her.

---

56 ABU 'ABDULLAH MUHAMMAD B. AL-MUJAHID[2]

A man learned in the sacred sciences and a jurist of the Mālikite school,[3] he taught at the Mosque of al-Muqaibirāt. He lived his life in accordance with the saying of the Prophet, on whom be blessings and peace, 'Reckon with yourselves before you are brought to the Reckoning.' Thus he would make a note of all his thoughts, actions, words, what he had heard and similar things. After the prayer of nightfall he would seclude himself in his room and go over all his actions of that day which demanded repentence and repented of them. He would do likewise with all that called for his gratitude. He would then compare all his actions with what was required of him by the sacred Law. Having done this he would sleep a little, after which he would rise to say his litanies (*wird*) and pray in accordance with the custom of the Prophet. Thus he would sleep and pray alternately throughout the night.[4]

He would make a circle of his books around him so that when

[1] This incident is also related in *Futūḥāt*, II, p. 348.

[2] All the following material is from the *Durrah*. Esad Ef. 1777, f. 76a.

[3] See above, p. 83, n. 4.

[4] Prayer at night is especially recommended both by the Qur'an (LXXIII, 1–7) and the Prophet, who himself spent much of the night in worship.

he had completed some devotion or act of worship, he would take up one of the books and read it to himself. One day the Caliph Abū Ya'qūb visited him.[1] During their conversation, the Caliph said to him, 'O 'Abdallāh, do you not find living on your own rather lonely?' He replied, 'Intimacy with God abolishes all loneliness; for how can I be alone when He is always present with me? Whenever I wish to converse with my Lord, may His majesty be exalted, I take up the Qur'an. Should I wish to converse with the Apostle of God, the peace and blessings of God be upon him, I take up a volume of the Traditions, and if I wish to commune with the Followers of the Prophet, I take up some work dealing with their lives. So it is with every one with whom I would converse. How then can you speak of loneliness, O Abū Ya'qūb?' He then recited some verses referring to this practice.

As Abū Ya'qūb was about to take his leave of him he ordered his door-keeper, Abū al-'Alā' b. Jāmi', to give the Shaikh something whereby to ameliorate his condition. The gift consisted of a box containing a thousand gold dinārs. When the Shaikh pointed out that he had no need of the money, the Caliph said that all apart from God had need of things. At this 'Abdallāh said, 'You are quite right, so why not return it to its owner who has more need of it than I', thus implying that it had been wrongfully acquired. When he heard this the Caliph blushed with shame and left the money in the middle of the room. The box remained where the Caliph had left it, unopened and unattended by the Shaikh for nearly twelve years until the Shaikh died. When the Sultan Abū Isḥāq b. Yūsuf[2] was told the story of the money he attended his funeral himself. Then something rather unusual happened: it was commanded that the money be paid to the needy members of the Shaikh's family according to their condition and not according to the normal rules of inheritance.

One day the Shaikh needed some money, but found that he had nothing but a ragged old mantle worth half a dirham which he gave to the broker to sell for him. When the broker told the people that the mantle belonged to Ibn al-Mujāhid one of the merchants bid as high as seventy gold dinars. Then

[1] Almohad Caliph (AD 1163–84).
[2] One of the sons of the above-mentioned Abū Ya'qūb.

the broker took the purchaser, the money and the mantle to the Shaikh. When the Shaikh asked what all the money was for, the broker explained that it was the price paid for the mantle. At this the Shaikh bowed his head and, with tears in his eyes, said, over and over again, 'So the religion of Ibn al-Mujāhid is worth seventy dinars!' Then he said to the merchant, taking back his mantle, 'This is not the true value of my mantle, my friend; I will not sell, so take back your money.' Then, in obedience to the Shaikh, the merchant took his money and left weeping. It is said that he then gave the money away as alms. After that God provided for the Shaikh's needs from an unexpected source.

One day, as he was returning to his house from the mosque, he noticed that someone unknown to him was following him. When he reached the door of his house he stopped and said to the man, 'You there! If you are in need of anything, speak out and tell me what it is.' The other replied that he needed nothing from him. Then the Shaikh went in to his house and locked the door, leaving the fellow outside. No sooner was he in the entrance hall than he saw that the man was in the house with him. He said to him, 'How did you get into the house, seeing that the door is locked and you did not ask permission to enter?' The man replied, 'O Shaikh, I am no man but an angel of the Lord sent to be with you and protect you from evil.' At this the Shaikh wept. The angel remained with him until the day of his death.

Most of his spiritual states have been dealt with in the *al-Durrat al-fākhirah*, of which this is a synopsis.[1] Many came to the Way through him including, Ibn Qassūm,[2] Abū 'Imrān al-Martūlī,[3] al-Shantarīnī and al-Aṣbaḥī, as also many of the righteous of Seville from all of whom I have benefited greatly.

---

57 ABU AL-HASAN AL-MUNHANALI[4]

He adhered most strictly to the canonical prayers, spoke to no one and kept company with none, being constantly occupied

[1] See Introduction. [2] See above, p. 83. [3] See above, p. 87.

[4] Esad Ef. 1777, f. 86a. Al-Munḥanālī is a conjectural reading, the manuscript being almost illegible at this point.

with the salvation of his soul. A man of lofty intellect, much given to sighs and wearing always a sorrowful countenance. He once fasted day and night for twenty-five days. He was most dutiful towards his mother.

I was one of his companions for nearly ten years. He never asked me where I had come from or where I was going. One day in the month of July he was sitting in the Friday mosque. Although the heat was intense he was smiling. When I asked him what cause he had to smile, he said, 'The heat is indeed intense, but God is kind to his servants.' Towards the late afternoon the rain began to fall and by the time of the prayer the heavens had opened and it rained so heavily that the streets ran in torrents.

---

58 AHMAD AL-SHARISHI[1] of Jerez

He was one of those who had been devoted to the worship of God since boyhood and was brought up by the Shaikh Abū Aḥmad b. Saidabūn.[2]

When he was only ten years of age or younger a spiritual state overcame him and he fell into a fire, but the fire did not harm him. We have seen this kind of thing happen in his case many times. We asked him whether he was aware of what happened to him on these occasions and he replied that he was not. He died in our company at Shu'b 'Alī and we buried him there in the year 608 H.

He once asked his father if he might leave him to go on the Pilgrimage. His father replied, 'My boy, I am your father and I wanted you for myself, and now you want to leave me and be off.' Aḥmad said, 'O my father, if you will be frank with me in answering a question, I will abide by what you say. When you lay with my mother did you intend my existence?' The father replied, 'No, my son, I did it only to satisfy my desire.' The son then said, 'God is the greatest, for He it was who created me and it is He Who summons me to His sacred House. Now, since I am able to do so, I have no excuse for delaying my journey,

[1] Esad Ef. 1777, f. 86a.

[2] See above, p. 19.

for my existence is not a gift bestowed by you but the gift of Him Who created me for His service.' At these words the father, who was a pious man, wept and gave his blessing to his son's intention.

Before leaving for the East he came to seek my advice on the Pilgrimage. I gave him my blessing. Two years later I met him again in Damascus where he stayed with me until he went to the mercy of God.

---

59 ABU 'ABDALLAH AL-GHILLIZI[1]

He was from the fortress of Ghillizah in Spain, a righteous man and utterly devoted to God.

One night, very late, a man knocked on his door calling for a piece of cow's liver; he went to the door to see who might want such a thing from him. Since he had a cow in his possession a voice within him said, 'We are only asking you for something you possess.' At this he recalled that he did indeed have a cow; so he took a knife, slaughtered the cow and gave its liver to the man at the door.

One day we were out walking with him near Seville when the time for the prayer came. This Shaikh of ours had not performed the ritual ablution. Then he noticed a man passing water close by, so he went to the place and performed his ablution in it. When I saw this I told the others to take no notice of this action, since the Shaikh was a true man and God is all-powerful. Then I told them to go and inspect the remains of the urine with which they had seen him perform the ablution and they found it to be sweet, untainted water. Then I said, 'He Who is able to turn wine into vinegar is just as able to turn urine into water.' Then we said the prayer.

One day, as he was travelling in Murcia, he passed by a man and his son in a garden quarrelling over some water for the plants. Seeing this the Shaikh wept and said, 'O Lord, the treasuries of the heaven are full and You are able to provide them, but You have caused this boy to be insolent to his father over a drop of water.' Hardly had he uttered these words than

[1] Esad Ef. 1777, f. 97a.

the heavens opened and the father and son were reconciled, having no more need of their own water.

The pangs of death afflicted him for fifteen days before he died. When he was able to speak towards the end of his agony he said, 'God has caused me to suffer the pangs of death for fifteen days in order to show me certain things I have committed in the past.' When he had mentioned what they were he said, 'Now I am on my way to my Lord; peace be upon you!' Then he uttered the creed (There is no god but God, and Muhammad is His Messenger), closed his eyes and departed this life.

---

60 'ABD AL-MAJID B. SALMAH[1]

This Shaikh was from Marchena of the Olives, a man devoted to the Qur'an and self-discipline. He served Shams, Mother of the Poor.[2] Many of the greatest Shaikhs benefited from her guidance, including 'Abdallāh al-Mawrūrī,[3] Aḥmad b. Qaiṭūn and Mu'ādh b. Ashras.

One night as he was praying on his prayer mat he sensed that someone had entered the room, although the door was locked. Immediately he rushed upon him. The other said to him, 'Do not try to frighten one who enjoys intimacy with God, for he cannot be disturbed,' Then he asked the man, 'Sir, by virtue of what attainments do the Substitutes hold their position?'[4] He replied, 'By the four which Abū Ṭālib al-Makkī mentioned in his *Sustenance of the Hearts*,[5] namely, hunger, wakefulness, silence and seclusion from men.' Then he took him by the hand and, leaving the house, took him during the space of that night to visit various places on earth, invoking God the while. When the first light came he returned him to his house and departed. He would come to see him from time to time, always at night. The name of his visitant was Mu'ādh b. Ashras who was considered to be one of the Substitutes.

[1] Esad Ef. 1777, f. 98a. Cf. *Ḥilyat al-abdāl*, Hyderabad, 1948, p. 3.

[2] See above, p. 142. [3] See above, p. 101. [4] See above, p. 115, n. 1.

[5] *Qūt al-qulūb* by al-Makkī is one of the most well-known of Sufi treatises. Al-Makkī died in AD 996.

61 ABU ISHAQ IBRAHIM AL-HINNAWI[1]
the Henna Collector

He lived in the city of Ronda and was one of the most prominent contemporaries of Ibrāhīm b. al-Ṭarīf.[2] He was a leading member and *muqaddam*[3] of the order of Chivalry.

One day as I was leaving him after a visit he came out with me to say farewell and to ask me to convey his greetings to the Shaikh Abū 'Abdallāh al-Qasṭīlī.[4] I was also to tell him that al-Ḥinnawī longed to see him again. When I had been on my way for a short while I heard a voice behind me calling me to stop. I turned round, saw the Shaikh and was about to go back to him, when he told me to stay where I was. When he reached me I saw that he was weeping. When I asked the cause of this he said, 'I am a liar myself and I have asked you to lie for me.' When I asked him what he meant he replied, 'If I really longed to see al-Qasṭīlī again I could easily do so, seeing that I am quite able to ride or walk to see him. You see what happens when I am lazy in watching over my soul.' He began to weep again until I forgave him and set off on my journey again.

62 AL-ASHALL AL-QABA'ILI[5]

One of the foremost of those devoted to the Qur'an, the Pole of his time.[6] He would visit us quite often, but would only discuss the Qur'an. At that time I knew nothing of his station.

One night, in a dream, I was told that this man was the Pole of the time, the fount of succour, the Imām (here the words are illegible). When I woke, al-Sammād, the righteous, summoned me on behalf of Ibn Ḥayyūn to go to his garden with a group of others, Al-Ashl was one of the company. When we reached the garden we all began to talk together. Then I remembered my vision and announced to the company, 'Last night I saw an

[1] Esad Ef. 1777, f. 99a.
[2] See above, p. 128.
[3] The deputy of a Shaikh.
[4] See above, p. 138.
[5] Esad Ef. 1777, f. 102a.
[6] See above, p. 115, n. 1.

amazing thing.' Then al-Ashall said to me, 'If you want to tell about your vision do not mention the subject's name to anyone.' I agreed to this. As we were leaving the Shaikh said to me, 'It is no longer good for me to stay in this town, now that you know who I am.' Then he bade me farewell and departed. I have never met him since.[1]

63 IBN AL-HAKIM AL-KAHHAL[2]

This man was a preacher in Tunis. We met quite by accident. One day I was standing in a place in which it is unlawful to be. As he passed by he said to me, 'You there! The likes of you does not stand in a place like that!' I must add that no-one knew of my state. I told him that I repented of it and he replied, 'The door of repentance is open.'

This Shaikh was the Imām and preacher at the Friday mosque, and when the muezzin, at the night prayer, heard him cough softly, he would open the prayer.[3] One night the cough was late in coming. Now Bashīr, the water-carrier, was out in courtyard when something fell on him from the sky; it was the Imām who immediately went into the mosque and coughed softly so that the muezzin opened the prayer. Later he told Bashīr to keep secret what he had seen till the day he died. When Bashīr asked him how he had come to be in the air and where he had been, the Imām told him that he had been in Mecca when the night prayer was called, but that he had only just started the first of his seven circumambulations of the Ka'bah, which was why he had been late for the prayer.[4]

The judge, Abū 'Abdallāh b. Darqah, who was the local governor, wanted to put him in charge of the treasury in which the wealth of orphans was deposited. The Shaikh himself wanted none of it, but feared that they would bring pressure to

[1] Cf. *Futūḥāt*, IV, p. 76. He was from Bugia. Ibn 'Arabī met him while staying in Fez in 593/1196 (see Introduction, p. 31).

[2] Esad Ef. 1777, f. 103b.

[3] At the beginning of a congregational prayer, someone other than the Imam repeats the call to prayer, with modifications, before the Imam leads the congregation in the prayer proper.

[4] The circumambulation of the Ka'bah is part of the rites of the Pilgrimage (*ḥājj*). Cf. *Encyclopaedia of Islam*, art. *Hadjdj*.

bear upon him to accept the post. On the other hand he would feel ashamed to reject it; so he tried to think of a plan to deflect them from choosing him. God then inspired him to put on his clothes and go to the citadel, where the men in power were. When he presented himself before them they asked him, with great respect, why he had come. He told them that he had heard that they wanted to put him in charge of the orphan's treasury. Then he made it look as if he could not wait to get his hands upon it. At this the others looked at one another and told him that he would be told about it later. Then they fell silent and he left them. When he had gone they decided that one so keen on the post was not fit to receive it.

64 A SLAVE GIRL OF QASIM AL-DAWLAH[1]

She belonged to our master the Prince of the Faithful. She lived in the neighbourhood of Mecca and died there. She was unique in her time and had attained the power to cover great distances quickly. When she was away on her wanderings she would commune with the mountains, rocks and trees, saying to them, 'Welcome, welcome!' Her spiritual state was strong and she served the Folk and followed the Way with unswerving sincerity. She had the virtues of chivalry and was most strenuous in self-discipline, frequently practising day-and-night fasting. Despite this she was strong and her exertions seemed to suit her well. I have never seen one more chivalrous than her in our time. Dedicated to the exaltation of God's majesty, she attached no worth to herself.

65 ZAINAB AL-QAL'IYYAH[2]

From the fortress of the Banū Jamād, she was of those devoted to the Book of God, the foremost ascetic of her day. Although she possessed both great beauty and considerable wealth she freely abandoned the world and went to live in the region of Mecca, a woman ennobled by God. I had contact with her both

[1] Esad Ef. 1777, f. 104a.

[2] Esad Ef. 1777, f. 104b.

in Seville and at Mecca. She was the companion of many eminent men of the Folk, among them, Ibn Qassūm,[1] al-Shubarbulī,[2] Maimūm al-Qirmizī, Abū al-Ḥusain b. al-Ṣā'igh,[3] a Traditionist and a notable ascetic, Abū al-Ṣabr Ayyūb al-Qahrī, and others.

When she sat down to practise Invocation she would rise into the air from the ground to a height of thirty cubits; when she had finished she would descend again.[4] I accompanied her from Mecca to Jerusalem and I have never seen anyone more strict in observing the times of prayer than her. She was one of the most intelligent people of her time.

66 ABU 'ABDALLAH AL-TARTUSI[5]

This man was of those devoted to the practice of Invocation. I met him at Tlemcen in the Maghrib. One day as I sat with him we talked about Abū Madyan.[6] As we talked it seemed to me that he was critical of Abū Madyan because of his illiteracy. This caused me to have certain reservations about him. That same night I saw the Apostle of God (may God bless him and grant him peace) in a dream. He said to me, 'O Muḥammad, your feelings have changed towards al-Ṭarṭūsī for the sake of Abū Madyan. How is it that you cannot love him for his love of God and His Apostle?' I replied, 'From now on, O Apostle, I will do as you say.' In the morning I took some gold and some fine clothes and presented them to al-Ṭarṭūsī and told him what I had seen. At this he wept and abandoned his critical attitude towards Abū Madyan and the whole affair was blessed by God's grace (*barakah*).[7]

67 IBN JA'FAR[8]

I met him in Africa and he treated me like a brother. His supplications were always answered and he was quite advanced on

[1] See above, p. 83. [2] See above, p. 79. [3] See above, p. 136.

[4] Levitation is one of the more familiar phenomena of mystical experience. Cf. Evelyn Underhill, *Mysticism*, pp. 376 f.

[5] Esad Ef. 1777, f. 105a. [6] See above, p. 69, n. 3.

[7] Cf. *Futūḥāt*, IV, p. 498. The meeting took place in 590/1193.

[8] Esad Ef. 1777, f. 105b.

the Way. Once, when he succumbed to some impurity, God punished him on the spot by causing his head to be stuck in the earth, his feet in the air. His back stuck out an arm's length. Although he cried for help, no one was able to pull him out. When the matter was reported to his Shaikh he came and ordered him to repent of his sin, which he did. Immediately his back returned to its place and the rest of his limbs were freed.[1]

One day he was standing with the Prince of the Faithful Yaḥyā b. Isḥāq;[2] this was at a time when the world was full of the noise of armies, drums and horns. He was smiling and when the Prince asked the reason for this he replied, 'At this monstrous business you are involved in. They will show you no honour, but will conspire to defeat you.'

At this the Prince wept and said, 'Yes indeed, for what you see are the Arabs of Africa.'

68 'UMAR AL-QARQARI[3]

A godly man dedicated to self-discipline, who preferred seclusion from men and sat with no-one. He earned his living with his own hands and of his earnings he took only what he needed for food, leaving the rest with his employer and saving nothing for the morrow.

When he came to this country he heard of us and came to visit us. When he came he sat with us in a fashion not customary among us. Some of the others remarked on this, so during the session I said to him, 'O 'Umar, if you wish to leave us, go!' At this he wept and said 'My brother, a gathering for the sake of God is something which ought to be taken full advantage of; therefore leave me out of it, for the session is useless for me if I am to be made conscious only of myself.'[4]

[1] Immediate punishment is, in a certain sense, an act of divine mercy in that one is immediately alerted to one's true state and, at the same time, delivered from future retribution, perhaps accumulated.

[2] Yaḥya b. Isḥāq was an Almoravid prince who continued to resist the Almohads long after their conquest of the Maghrib and southern Spain. For some years he held territories in the region of Tunis. He died in AD 1237.

[3] Esad Ef. 1777, f. 105b.

[4] During a *majlis* one's whole concentration should be on God, not on oneself or others. This Shaikh, unused as he was to the company of others, had, by his awkwardness, diverted his own attention and that of the others from the remembrance of God.

I heard him say, 'Man must worship in seclusion in this world and not come out of it except into the next world.' He asked me to give him one of my garments, so I gave him a striped piece of clothing I had. I later heard that he had been wrapped in it when he died.

---

69 'ALI IBN 'ABDALLAH B. JAMI'[1]

He was a man dedicated to self-discipline, a servant of 'Alī al-Mutawakkil and others. I went once to return a visit he had made to me. When I got to his house, he had me sit down in a particular spot in the room. When I asked the reason for this he replied, that al-Khiḍr[2] had sat there and that he had put me there because of the spiritual power still adhering to it. Then he went on to tell me what had happened during al-Khiḍr's visit. He said, 'Although I had not mentioned the *khirqah*,[3] he brought out a small cotton cap and placed it with his own hands on my head. I then took it off, kissed it and placed it between him and me. Then he said to me, "O 'Alī, would you like me to invest you with the *khirqah*?" I replied, "O Master, who am I to say?" Then he took it in his hands in another way and put it on my head.' Then I said to 'Alī, 'Do with me as he did with you.' Then he took a small cloth cap and performed exactly the same ceremony with me. I myself have always performed this investiture in accordance with the tradition passed down through the chain of spiritual masters (*silsilah*),[4] and it is the way in which I invest others with the *khirqah*.[5]

[1] Esad Ef. f. 108a. Cf. *Futūḥāt*, I, pp. 186–7. He met this Shaikh in Mosul, Iraq, in 601/1204.

[2] Al-Khiḍr features in the Qur'an (XVIII, 65–82) together with Moses, where al-Khidr represents the esoteric knowledge or gnosis (*'ilm ladunnī*) and Moses the exoteric dispensation (*sharī'ah*). Although He seems to have no historical identity he has been associated with legends concerning Gilgamesh and Alexander, as also Enoch. For the Sufis he is the prototype and patron of Saints (*awliyā'*). See *Encyclopaedia of Islam*, art. *Khaḍir*.

[3] The *khirqah* or 'ragged mantle' is the token of initiation into the Way of the Sufis. Initiation by al-Khiḍr himself is the highest kind, which the author himself received. Cf. *Encyclopaedia of Islam*, art. *Khirḳah*.

[4] The *silsilah* is the series of spiritual masters through whom a Sufi traces his spiritual ancestry by initiation. It is rather like a spiritual genealogy. Cf. M. Lings, *A Sufi Saint of the Twentieth Century*, London, 1971, Appendix B.

[5] See above, p. 39.

70 'ABD AL-HAQQ AL-HABDAMIWI AL-WARRAQ[1]

A righteous man who enjoyed revelations and was always truthful in his dealings, he once visited Jerusalem with his household and then wished to return to Fawwā (Qawwā?), but his wife refused to accompany him because she wished to stay in Jerusalem. He nevertheless insisted on returning to Fawwā so that he might end his days there. Then he told her that the Franks would come and take over Jerusalem and take her captive. Then she would go to Acre, but she would return to Jerusalem where she would die. Everything happened exactly as he had foretold. In 598 H. I also met his brother, Abū 'Abdallāh al-Ḥabdamīwī al-Gharbī, who now lives at al-Kalāsah.

71 'ABDALLAH BADR AL-HABASHI The Servant[2]

He was my companion for twenty-three years and died while I was with him at Malatya. He had also been a companion to Abū Zakariyā' al-Bajā'ī at Ma'arrah, Abū al-Ḥasan b. al-Shakkāl al-Fāsī at Aleppo, Rabī' b. Maḥmūd al-Māridīnī al-Khaṭṭāb, Abū 'Abdallāh b. Ḥasan and in the Maghrib, Ismā'īl al-Raqrāqī, a great man who lived near the Sanctuary at Mecca and was hurt in its collapse (?). He had been my companion in the Maghrib. Then al-Habashi came to the Maghrib and was my companion in Fez.

When death came to him at my house he was quite willing and ready to meet his Lord. He died in the night. I myself had intended to wash his body. However, in the morning the people came to pay their respects and among them was the righteous jurist Kamāl al-Dīn Muẓaffar, a man of the town and one of the Folk. When I explained about the washing he exclaimed, 'God is the greatest', and was overcome by a spiritual state. When I

[1] Esad Ef. 1777, f. 111a.

[2] See above, p. 119. At the beginning of the *Ḥilyat al-abdāl* in *Rasā'il Ibnul Arabī* (Hyderabad, 1948) al-Habashī is described as the freedman of Abū al-Ghanā'im b. Abū al-Futūḥ al-Ḥarrānī.

asked him about it he told me, 'Yesterday, when I was in my garden a voice told me to wash myself, to which I replied that I had no need to do so. The request was made three times and after the third time I was told to be ready to wash the body of one of God's servants on the morrow. Then I went to wash myself in the brook which runs through the garden. Indeed I had no idea who had died until you summoned me here and told me to wash him.' Then he began to wash al-Ḥabashī's body. When he had completed his task I asked him to lead the prayer. When we had finished the prayer he told me that when he was beginning to wash the body and thinking how unworthy he was to wash such a man, the eyes of al-Ḥabashī opened, looked up at him, smiled and then closed again.

I myself went to his grave during the afternoon and complained to him of something which had befallen me after his death. He answered me from his grave and gave praise to God. I heard his voice clearly as he expressed concern for what I had told him, may God rest his soul.

The preacher Badr al-Dīn told me at Malatya on the authority of some of his household that they had looked down by night from the rooftop on to the grave of al-Ḥabashī and had seen a great light reaching to it from the sky. The light had persisted until dawn.[1]

OTHER SHAIKHS

FROM 'AL-DURRAT AL-FAKHIRAH'

I also met, at Cordova; Yūsuf b. Sakhr, who was considered to be one of the Substitutes[2] and gifted with the power of prophecy; also Abdallāh al-Shakkāz at Granada, one of the greatest of those who strive (for perfection);[3] also Abū Aḥmad b. Saidabūn at Wādī Ashth, a great Shaikh from eastern Spain[4] and an equal with Aḥmad al-Rifā'ī at al-Baṭā'iḥ who was also on the Way. Al-Rifā'ī was a stocky man.[5] I was told of this in Damas-

[1] Here the sketches end with a long list of other persons whom he met during the course of his life.

[2] See above, p. 115. [3] See above, p. 110. [4] See above, p. 119.

[5] The manuscript reads *rab' rajulin.*

cus by Shaikh 'Atīq al-Lurqī who had it from Abū 'Abdallāh Qaḍīb al-Bān who was a just witness.[1] At Qasr Kutāmah[2] I met 'Abd al-Jalīl, a member of the People of Faith,[3] and Abū Aḥmad, one of the righteous and the elect. At Bugia I met Abū Zakariyā' al-Zawāwī al-Ḥasanī, one of the Banū Ḥasan in the Maghrib, a most humble scholar. I met Abū al-'Abbās al-Muḥsin when he was weak with age, although his faith was strong and his veracity untainted. Among them also was Ibn 'Umar, the reciter at Tunis and a man devoted to the Qur'ān;also Muḥammad al-Nābilī and al-Ḥājj 'Abdallāh al-Nābilī, also al-Rajabī al-Khaṭarī (?) at Dunaisir, who was one of the forty Rajabis who uttered wondrous things in the month of Rajab and became like other men when the month was over;[4] also 'Abdallāh al-Qaḍḍāb, who fled to the mountain (seeking seclusion) before he had reached maturity. I met al-Sammād al-Tawsilī (?) whose name was 'Abdallāh, a companion of 'Abdallāh al-Ḥawwārī. I met Abū 'Abdallāh al-Hawwārī at Mecca where he died in the year 600/1203. One day in Mecca I met seventy-two of the saints from all of whom I witnessed miraculous powers. I also met a large group of both men and women, remarkable for their spiritual power and knowledge.

[1] See above, p. 128. [2] See above, p. 64, n. 2.

[3] The Arabic reads *shā'b al-īmān*. It is not clear what is meant by these words.

[4] See above, p. 41.

Bibliography

AFIFI, A. A., *The Mystical Philosophy of Muhid Din Ibnul Arabi*, Cambridge, 1939.

AL-BALAWAĪ, YŪSUF B. MUḤAMMAD, *Kitāb alif bā'*, Būlāq, 1286 H.

BARGÈS, J. J. J., *Vie du celèbre marabout Cidi Abou Medien*, Paris, 1884.

BLOCHET, E. 'Ètudes sur l'esoterisme musulman', *Journal Asiatique*, XX, 1902, pp. 528 ff., and XX, 1902, pp. 49 ff.

BROCKELMANN, C., *Geschichte der arabischen Literatur*, 2 vols, Leyden, 1943–9; Supplement, 2 vols, 1937–42.

AL-BUKHĀRĪ, MUḤAMMAD B. ISMA'ĪL, *Saḥīḥ*; 3 vols ed. by L. Krehl, Leyden, 1862–8; vol. 4 by T. Juynboll, 1907–8.

BURCKHARDT, T., *An Introduction to Sufi Doctrine*, Lahore, 1959.

CORBIN, H., *L'Imagination créatrice dans le soufisme d'Ibn Arabī*, Paris, 1958.

DA'ŪD, ABŪ, *Sunan*, 2 vols, Cairo, 1292 H.

Encyclopaedia of Islam, 4 vols, Leyden, 1913–34.

AL-FALAḤ, ABŪ 'ABD AL-ḤAYY, 'The Lives of 'Umar Ibnul-Farid and Muhyyuddin Ibnul-Arabi', ed. by R. A. Nicholson in *Journal of the Royal Asiatic Society*, 1906, pp. 816 ff.

GARDET, L. and ANAWATI, G., *Mystique musulmane*, Paris, 1961.

GHAZĀLĪ, ABŪ ḤĀMID, *Iḥya 'ulūm al-dīn*, 4 vols, Cairo, 1939.

AL-HAJJĀJ, MUSLIM B., *Saḥīḥ*, 18 vols, in 6, Cairo, 1349 H.

ḤUJWĪRĪ, 'ALĪ B. 'UTHMĀN, *Kashf al-maḥjūb*, trans. by R. A. Nicholson, London, 1911.

IBN ABBĀR, MUḤAMMAD B. 'ABDALLĀH, *Takmilah*, ed. by F. Codera, 2 vols, Madrid, 1887–9.

IBN 'ARABĪ, MUḤAMMAD B. 'ALĪ, 'Autobibliografia de Ibn Arabī', ed. by A. Badawi in *Al-Andalus*, XX, 1955, pp. 107–28.

—— *al-Durrat al-fākhirah*, MS. Esad Ef., Instanbul. 1777.

—— *Fuṣūṣ al-ḥikam*, ed. by A. A. Afifi, Cairo, 1946; trans. by T. Burckhardt, *Sagesse des prophètes*, Paris, 1955.

—— *al-Futūḥāt al-Makkiyya*, Cairo, 1329 H.

—— *Ḥilyat al-abdāl*, trans. by M. Valsan, Paris, 1951.

—— *Kitāb al-khalwah*, MS Aya Sofya, Istanbul, 1644.

—— *Kleinere Schriften des Ibn Al-Arabī*, ed. by H. S. Nyberg, Leyden, 1919.

—— 'Memorandum by Ibn 'Arabī of His Own Works', ed. by A. A. Afifi in *Bulletin of the Faculty of Arts* (of Alexandria University), VIII, 1954, pp. 109–17.

—— *Muḥāḍarāt al-abrār*, Cairo, 1324 H.

—— *Nasab al-khirqah*, MS. Esad Ef., Istanbul, 1507. 87–97b.

—— *Rasā'il Ibn al-Arabī*, Hyderabad, 1948.

—— *Rūḥ al-quds*, MS. Istanbul University. 74A, 1–103. Damascus, 1964.

—— *Sharḥ khal' al-na'lain*, MS. Yusuf Aga, 5624, Eski. 109–338.
—— *Tarjumān al-aswāq*, Beirut, 1961.
IBN AL-'ARĪF, AHMAD B. MUḤAMMAD, *Maḥāsin al-majālis*, ed. by Asin Palacios, Paris, 1933.
IBN AL-ATHĪR, AL-MUBĀRAK B. MUHAMMAD, *Chronicon*, ed. by C. Tornberg, 1851–76.
IBN ̣ANBAL, AHMAD, *Musnad*, 11 vols, Cairo, 1949–53.
AL-JĪLĪ, 'ABD AL-KARĪM, *De l'Homme Universelle*, trans. by T. Burckhardt, Paris, 1953.
KADLOUBOVSKY, D. and PALMER, G. E. H., *Early Fathers from the Philokalia*, London, 1954.
LEVI-PROVENCAL, E., *La penisule Iberique au moyen-age*, Leyden, 1938.
LINGS, M., *A Sufi Saint of the Twentieth Century*, London, 1971.
AL-MAKKĪ, ABŪ ṬĀLIB, *Qūt al-qulūb*, 2 vols, Cairo, 310 I H.
MAQARRĪ, AḤMAD, *Analectes sur l'histoire et la litterature des Arabes*, ed. by R. Dozy, 2 vols, Amsterdam, 1965.
MEIER, F., 'The Mystery of the Ka'aba', *The Mysteries* (Papers from the Eranos Yearbooks II), New York, 1955.
AL-MUḤĀSIBĪ, HĀRITH B. ASAD, *Sharḥ al-ma'rifah*, MS British Museum, Or. 4026.
MUNAJJID, SALĀḤ AL-DĪN, *Manāqib Ibn 'Arabī*, Beirut, 1959.
NASR, S. H., *Three Muslim Sages*, Harvard, 1964.
NICHOLSON, R. A., *Studies in Islamic Mysticism*, Cambridge, 1921.
PALACIOUS, M. ASIN, *Islam Cristianizado*, Madrid, 1931.
al-Qur'an, Būlāq, 1342 H.
QUSHAIRĪ, 'ABD AL-KARĪM, *al-Risālah*, Cairo, 1940.
RŪMĪ, JALĀL AL-DĪN, *The Mathnawi*, trans. by R. A. Nicholson, London, 1925–40.
SCHUON, F., *Understanding Islam*, London, 1963.
—— 'The Nature and Function of the Spiritual Master', *Studies in Comparative Religion*, I, 1967, pp. 50–9.
SIRĀJ AL-DĪN, ABŪ BAKR, 'The Origins of Sufism', *Islamic Quarterly*, III, 1956, pp. 53–64.
TIRMIDHĪ, MUHAMMAD B, ĪSA, *Saḥīḥ*, 2 vols, Cairo, 1937.
UNDERHILL, E., *Mysticism*, London, 1930.
YAHYA, O., *Histoire et classification de l'oeuvre d'Ibn Arabī*, 2 vols, Damascus, 1964.

Index of Arabic Terminology

General Index

'Abd al-Jabbār, 36
'Abd al-Jalīl, 160
'Abd al-Karīm, 30
'Abd al-Mu'min, 78
'Abd al-Raḥīm, 101, 104
'Abd al-Razzāq, 101
'Abd al-Salām, 117
Ablution, 32, 39, 56, 74, 81, 83, 85 f., 127, 150, 158 f.
Abraham, 74
Absolute Reality, 54
Abstinence, 54
Abū al-'Abbās (of Ceuta), 33
Abū 'Abdallāh (the Almoravid), 140
Abū Aḥmad, 160
Abū al-'Alī, 129
Abū 'Āmir, 144
Abū Ḥanīfah (al-Nu'mān), 83
Abū al-Ḥasan (of Bugia), 39
Abū Madyan (Shu'aib), 27, 69, 71 f., 82, 101 f., 108, 115, 121 f., 127, 135, 141, 155
Abū Marwān, 102
Abū Najā, 101, 104, 128
Abū al-Qāsim, 30
Abū Sa'īd, 33
Abū Ya'izz, 132
Abū Ya'qūb Yūsuf, 22, 75, 129, 147
Acre, 158
'Ād, 124
Adam, 34, 73, 124
'Adawī (Ṣāliḥ), 73 ff., 96
Afifi (A.A), 31, 45, 47, 86, 133
Africa, 155 f.
Alarcos (Battle of), 29
'Alawī (Aḥmad), 53, 57
Alcala la real, 139
Aleppo, 40, 43 ff., 158
Alexander, 157
Alexandria, 36, 69, 107
Algarve, 26, 68
Algeciras, 128
Algeria, 69
'Alī (b. Abū Tālib), 74
Aljarafe, 76 ff.,
Almeria, 32, 101 f., 104
Almohads, 21 f., 27, 29, 32 f., 78, 114, 129, 147, 156
Almonteber, 71, 79
Almoravids, 26, 156
Alms, 69
Anatolia, 43
Anqā' mughrib, 133
al-Andalus, 22
Andalusia, 25 ff., 29, 33, 63, 119
Anger, 119
Antioch (Battle of), 43
Apostle, 67, 112
'Arabī (Abū 'Abdallāh), 34
'Arafāt, 74
Archives Marocaines, 64
Armenia, 41
Arzan, 41
Aṣbaḥi, 148
Asia Minor, 39 f.
Aspiration, 53
Aswad ('Abd al-Salām), 138
Atlantic Ocean, 131
Attributes (of God), 109
Audition, 66
'Awārif al-ma'ārif, 42
Awqaf Library, 40
Aya Sofya Library, 79
Azdī ('Abd al-Wahhāb), 38, 107
Azhar Mosque (Fez), 30

Badawi (A.), 22
Badr al-Dīn, 159
Baghdad, 38, 41 f., 48, 87
Baghdādī (al-Qārī), 114
Bāghī (Abū 'Abdallāh), 134
Bajā'ī (Abū Zakariyā'), 158
Bājī (Abū 'Abdallāh), 136
Balawī (Yūsuf), 87, 91

Fāsī (Abū al-Ḥasan), 158
Fasting, 24, 56, 85, 91 f., 97, 111, 117, 134, 149, 154
Fatih Library, 36
al-Fātiḥah, 145
Fāṭimah (bint Ibn al-Muthannā), 25 f., 65, 143 ff.
Fāṭimah (bint Yūnus), 46
Fawwā, 158
Fear (of God), 138
Fennel, 77 f.
Fez, 29 ff., 34, 37, 69, 76, 114 f., 122, 132, 135, 139, 153, 158
Fihris al-muṣannafāt, 19
Folk, 23, 96, 106, 154, 155, 158
Food, 118, 130
Franks, 137, 158
Freethinkers, 106
Friday Prayer, 89, 117
Fuṣūṣ al-ḥikam, 38, 41, 45, 47 f., 86
al-Futūhāt al-Makkiyyah, 21 ff., 23, 25 ff., 63, 65, 69, 76, 79, 83, 87, 89, 99, 101, 103, 107 ff., 116, 122, 128 ff., 133 ff., 140, 142 f., 146, 153, 155, 157

Gharbī (Abū 'Abdallāh), 158
Ghazālī (Abū Ḥāmid), 51, 136 f.
Ghazzāl (Abū 'Abdallāh), 32, 101 f.
Ghazzāl (Abū 'Abdallāh), 32, 101 f., 104
Ghillizah, 150
Ghilīzī (Abū 'Abdallāh), 150 f.
Gilgamesh, 157
Gnosis, 134 f., 157
God (Allāh), 51 ff., *et passim*
Goitre, 128
Grace (divine), 53, 55, 66, 88, 122, 139
Granada, 32, 102, 110, 139, 159
Guilds, 129
Guru, 58

Ḥabashī ('Abdallāh), 69, 86, 88, 103, 110, 114, 119, 128, 158 f.
Ḥaddād, 134
Hamadan, 45
Ḥamral (Mosque of), 133
Hanbalites (Wall of), 141
Ḥarīrī (Aḥmad), see al-Jarrār
Harran, 41, 158
Ḥarrānī (Abū al-Ghanā'im), 158
Hārūn (Shaikh), 111
Ḥasan (Hospice of), 117
Ḥasanī (Yaḥyā), 137, 160
Ḥaṣār (Abū al-'Abbās), 31
Ḥaṣār (Muḥammad), 34, 36
Ḥawwārī ('Abdallāh), 160
Healing, 134
Heart, 56
Hebron, 39
Heedlessness, 26, 55, 131
Henna, 115, 152
Hesychasts, 68
Ḥilyat al-abdāl, 38, 48, 151, 158
Hinduism, 54, 122, 143
Ḥinnāwī (Ibrāhīm), 152
Histoire et classification de l'oeuvre d'Ibn Arabī, 17 ff., 47 f.
Hope, 6
Hūd, 124
Ḥudaibiyah, 58
Ḥujwīrī ('Alī), 33, 51, 65 f., 70, 81, 88 f., 91 f., 106, 111
Hunger, 151

Ibn Abbār (Muḥammad), 73, 79, 83, 101, 135
Ibn 'Abd al-Jalīl, 128
Ibn 'Abdūn (Muḥammad), 22
Ibn Abū al-Faḍl (Muḥammad), 109
Ibn al-'Arabī ('Abdallāh), 99 f.
Ibn al-'Arabī ('Alī), 21 f., 99 f., 114
Ibn 'Arabī (Muḥyi al-Dīn), 21 ff., *et passim*
Ibn al-'Arīf (Aḥmad), 32, 66, 101, 104
Ibn Ashras (Mu'ādh), 151
Ibn Assāl ('Abdallāh), 124
Ibn al-Athīr ('Alī), 94
Ibn Darqah (Abū 'Abdallāh), 153
Ibn Ghafīr (Abū al-Qāsim), 89 f.
Ibn Ghazūn (Abū al-'Alā'), 75
Ibn al-Ḥājj (Muḥammad), 117